Beyond the Bamboo

"For four years we were in the hands of a lot of lunatics: for us it was a medieval war. It couldn't have been more horrible. We were faced with death and brutality of the most extraordinary kind; we were utterly powerless minute by minute. That was a war within a war."

Laurens van der Post

To my wife, Iris

Also by Tom McGowran OBE:

Newhaven-on-Forth: Port of Grace, John Donald Publishers Ltd
Edinburgh, 1985.

ISBN 0 85976 130 4
Price £10.00
This history of Newhaven covers over four hundred and fifty years. The
author's own connections with the port prompted him to delve into the history
of Newhaven and the result of his painstaking research is a fascinating blend of
historical facts and amusing anecdotes which combine to provide a complete
picture of the folk who have lived there over the years. The book provided the
inspiration and framework for the setting up of a local museum.

Beyond the Bamboo Screen

Scottish Prisoners of War under the Japanese

Extracts from Newsletters of the Scottish Far East Prisoner of War Association and Other Sources

Compiled by Tom McGowran OBE

Cualann Press

ISBN 0 9535036 1 5

First Edition 1999

British Library Cataloguing in Publication Data. A catalogue record of this book is available at the British Library.

Printed by Bell & Bain, Glasgow

Beyond the Bamboo Screen is the second book in the *Voices of War* series published by:
Cualann Press, 6 Corpach Drive, Dunfermline, Fife, Scotland
Email cualann@ouvip.com **Website http://users.ouvip.com/cualann/**

Acknowledgements

I am grateful to the many contributors to *POW WOW*, the newsletter of the Scottish Far East Prisoner of War Association, whose writings appear in these pages.

Stanley Gimson QC, Chairman of the Scottish Far East Prisoner of War Association, provided sketches which were hidden in a sealed bottle and buried in the cemetery at Chungkai in April 1944. They were dug up in August 1945 and handed over to him in hospital in Rangoon none the worse for wear - which is more than could be said for him! For writing the Foreword and providing sketches, I am very grateful to Stanley.

I am also grateful for permission to publish received from:
John R Harris: 'Four George Crosses Won in Hong Kong';
Mrs Patricia Holmes: 'Internment Ditties' by John L Woods;
Mrs Sally Parkinson: 'Afterthoughts' by Dr A Graham;
The Baronage Press & Web Magazine, *Bamboo Shoots:* William Dennenberg's poem 'Was this Bushido?';
The Scotsman: 'Japanese A-Bomb' by Peter McGill, 1995
Jack B Chalker: watercolour and map from *Burma Railway Artist: The War Drawings of Jack Chalker,* published by Leo Cooper.

Particular thanks are due to Dennis W Carter for help with research.

I would also like to express my gratitude to the following:

John Murray (Publishers) Ltd: opening quotation from Laurens van der Post's *The Admiral's Baby;* Premedia Enthusiasts Publications USA: extracts from *World War II Magazine;* Jack B Edwards OBE: quotations from *Banzai You Bastards;* Bill Holtham: quotations from *Fulcrum,* the magazine of the Japanese Labour Camp Survivors' Association; Alan Matthews: information from *The Ship that Doomed a Colony.*

To all those named above and to many others responsible for war reports and publications referred to within the covers of this book, I am deeply indebted.

Tom McGowran

Illustrations

Sketches and photographs by G S Gimson

The sketches of camps by G S Gimson were drawn on the spot (except for 'Dysentery Ward, Kanyu Camp', to which the figures were added post-war). At first he sketched openly but when it became clear that the Japanese were becoming paranoid about security, he then sketched secretly with friends acting as lookouts. In April 1944, the risks involved in being found with even blank paper made it unwise to continue. With other papers, the sketches were inserted in a wine bottle, and buried, along with the records of one of the regiments, in an identifiable spot in Chungkai Camp Cemetery. After the Japanese surrender the regiment sent a squad to dig up the bottles and the sketches were returned to the artist.

Selarang Barrack Square, Changi, 1st - 5th September 1942   28
Kanyu Camp, Kiver Kwai, 14th March 1943   33
Chungkai Camp Hospital: Skin Wards   39
Wampo: The Largest Viaduct on the Line (post-war photo)   47
Train Journey, Singapore to Thailand, 28 December 1942   51
Tamarkan Bridge 5th April 1943   55
Chungkai Camp Distillery   67
Chungkai Camp: Bamboo Artificial Leg   71
Tamarkan Bridge (post-war photo by G S Gimson)   74
Chungkai Camp: In Hospital with all Belongings   82
Constructing the Railway: Cutting at Chungkai Camp (post-war photo)   85
Typical Insects (sketched post-war)   111
Chungkai Camps: New Operating Theatre, 1944   119
Dysentery Ward, Kanyu Camp   123
Final (Officers') Camp, Nakom Nayok   129
View from Tail-board of Lorry leaving Nakom Nayok Camp on
Journey to the Free World   132
Nakom Nayok Camp after the Japanese Surrender   133
Chungkai Camp Cemetery Spring 1944   151

Other Illustrations

Map of Burma and Thailand (Jack B Chalker)   16
Singapore's Final Hours (impression Tom McGowran)   17
Preparing the Trace in Bamboo Jungle (watercolour by Jack B Chalker)   61
Boon Pong & Brothers, Bangkok Today (photo Tom McGowran)   73
Mergui and Borneo Marches (impression by Tom McGowran)   87
Lisbon Maru   99
Peggy   117
Thin Men (source unknown)   139

Contents

FOREWORD 9

INTRODUCTION: THE WAR IN MALAYA 11

PART I: FALL OF EMPIRE 17

ARGYLLS IN ACTION *18*
THE DYING THROES *20*
ESCAPE FROM SINGAPORE *24*
CHANGI JAIL DITTY *30*

PART II: POW CAMPS 33

FOUR GEORGE CROSSES FOR HONG KONG *34*
MORE MEMORIES OF ARGYLE STREET *37*
WAS IT BUSHIDO? *40*
LOCKED IN A LAVATORY *42*
A CHILD IN CHINA *44*

PART III: THE THAI-BURMA RAILWAY 47

JAPANESE HOLIDAY *48*
THE THAI-BURMA RAILWAY *52*
AFTERTHOUGHTS *62*
LEE SOON (ALIAS BOON PONG) *72*
THE BEST OF ENEMIES *75*
INTELLIGENCE BEHIND BAMBOO *77*
SMILES *83*
COMPENSATION *86*

PART IV: MERGUI AND BORNEO 87

THE ROAD TO MERGUI *88*
BORNEO DEATH MARCH *95*
    JAP GERM WARFARE *98*

PART V: SHIPS AND MINES **99**

SINKING OF THE LISBON MARU *100*
THE HELL-SHIP THAT SAILED FROM KOWLOON *103*
1100 POWs DROWNED *105*
THE AWU MARU *107*
IRUKU COPPER MINES *108*
BANZAI YOU BASTARDS *109*

PART VI: PESTS AND PETS **111**

PESTS AND PETS *112*
PEGGY *116*
LUDWIG THE SAUSAGE DOG *118*

PART VII: THE CLOSING DAYS **123**

THE LAST MOVE *124*
JOURNEY'S END *129*
   THE FINAL SOLUTION *134*
OPERATION RANGOON JAIL *135*
SAVED FROM FRIENDLY FIRE *137*

PART VIII: THE JAPANESE SURRENDER **139**

   THE ATOM BOMBS *140*
POWs SAW BOMB DROPPED *141*
   PLANE CRASHED CARRYING POWS *143*
HOW THE GOOD NEWS CAME TO SOME *144*
   THE JAPANESE SURRENDER *145*
THEN HIROSHIMA HAPPENED *146*

PART IX: POST MORTEM **151**

INNOCENTS OF HIROSHIMA: EXPLODING THE MYTH *152*
   THE MANHATTAN PROJECT *154*
JAPANESE A-BOMB *155*
   JAPAN'S EXPERIMENTAL BOMB *158*
CHANGI EVENSONG *159*

Foreword

G S Gimson QC, LL D, Chairman, Scottish Far East POW Association

To anyone coming to these stories for the first time, the battles for Malaya and Singapore and the captivity and internment that followed will probably seem a crazy nightmare. Indeed they were. Looking back on the whole experience, the significant aspects for servicemen seem to me to have been the combined effects of overwork, severe malnutrition, tropical diseases, the almost indescribable squalor and the steady toll of deaths - but all these seen in light of the fact that we lived for over three years under threat, and without any really meaningful contact with homes and families or assurance of their continuing safety. For civilians, things were no doubt less extreme, but there were the anxieties caused by the separation of husbands and wives, what must have been the searing anxiety of watching children grow up in the unnatural surroundings of internment, lack of medicines and exposure to risks to health, plus, surely, the perpetual realisation for the women of their own vulnerability.

For several years after the end of the war little was generally known about prisoners' experiences in areas other than the Burma-Siam Railway. The earliest books *(eg Railroad of Death* by John Coast and *Naked Island* by Russell Braddon) dealt with that 'campaign'. The impression that it was the only significant experience was reinforced by the film *Bridge over the River Kwai*, hopelessly unrealistic though that was. In fact, the railway did account for the largest number of slave-labourers among POWs and the largest number of deaths in any one episode. Unhappily it also claimed the lives of uncounted thousands of native labourers, some accompanied by wives and children, sent there by the Japanese without proper administration or medical support, and with no effective understanding of hygiene. Their story will probably never be told.

Gradually, as Far East prisoners of war and civilians overcame their doubts about 'going public' - or indeed, their feeling that much of their story was scarcely fit to print - the flow of books increased from a trickle to a spate, so that there are now over 250 books including straightforward personal narratives, histories, military commentaries and even some works of fiction which are generally closely based on actual experiences. There was also the admirable TV serial *Tenko*. Some of these stories appear in this collection.

It scarcely needs to be said that the attitude of the Japanese Army of those days was based on utter contempt for servicemen who surrendered, an attitude expressed in brutality, callousness and almost universal lack of anything we would reckon as human feeling, The civilians were no doubt spared the worst excesses of this attitude, but they can never have felt safe. The 'ultimate disposal' planned by the Japanese Army involved the elimination of all military prisoners. The plan was only frustrated a matter of days before it was due to take place when Japan surrendered following the dropping of the atom bombs. In contrast, it should never be forgotten that, shortly before the end, on at least three occasions, POWs in transit, meeting wounded and sick Japanese soldiers who were given no assistance or comfort by their own personnel, pushed past the POWs own sentries to help and relieve the Japanese casualties. I saw one such incident and two others are well recorded.

You will readily understand that after all these experiences there is an unusually strong bond of fellowship among the survivors. Our various clubs and associations try to keep in touch, to give information on available welfare to all who may need it, and generally to provide occasions when the survivors can relax, exchange reminiscences, and know that their tales will be understood. A great part of the clubs' effectiveness lies in the regular publication of their newsletters including our *POW WOW* on which Tom McGowran has done such a fine job, nobly carrying on this essential service from his editorial ancestors.

Stanley Gimson

Introduction
THE WAR IN MALAYA

Tom McGowran OBE

Churchill called the war in Malaya the greatest reverse in the history of British Arms. What he failed to add was that he himself, for sound strategic reasons, had largely dictated the outcome.

In 1937 the Chiefs of Staff had issued a report estimating that the size of fleet required to safeguard Singapore in the event of war with Japan would be ten battleships and two battle cruisers with attendant escorts of cruisers and destroyers. Seventy days would be required to gather and send the fleet.

When Churchill came to power he asked the Chiefs of Staff to re-evaluate the position. They agreed that since the navy could not be spared to defend the colony, both it and Malaya were doomed and the only hope was to try to appease Japan in order to avert an attack. Churchill decided their revised report was so pessimistic that it must not be released and he continued to assert to the world that Singapore was an impregnable fortress. But it was decided to send a copy of the report to Sir Robert Brooke Popham, Commander in Chief Far East. For some unknown reason it was sent by a merchant ship, the *Automedon*.

On 11th November 1940, steaming through the Indian Ocean, the *Automedon* was attacked by the German raider *Atlantis* and laid dead in the water. The Germans boarded her, found the safe and blew it open. They removed two sacks labelled 'Safe Hand. British Master Only'. The German skipper, realising the importance of his find, informed Berlin.

The German interpretation of the find was: 'Churchill's Cabinet has decided the British are unable to send a fleet to the Far East and so must avoid 'open clash' with Japan until military co-operation with the United States is assured. The British will not go to war even if Japan attacks Thailand or Indo-China. Instead efforts will be made to buy off Tokyo with general concessions - including abandoning Singapore and Hong Kong and making a deal over Malaya (*The Ship that Doomed a Colony*). Hitler insisted that the Japanese be given a copy of the report. The Japanese, at first sceptical, were finally convinced it was genuine. Therefore, a year before the outbreak of the Far East war, Japan knew Great Britain could not defend her colonies. When one of the seamen aboard the *Automedon* escaped from a German prison camp and made his way back to Britain, the British became aware that the report had reached enemy hands.

With the sinking of the *Bismark* in October 1941 it at last became feasible to send a sizeable fleet to the Far East. This however Churchill forbade. He had absolutely no intention of attempting a defence of the indefensible. He would instead use the island as live bait to lure the Japanese into conflict. Churchill told his son Randolph that he would drag the United States into the war. So that it would not appear to the Americans that he had abandoned Singapore to its fate, he continued to send in troops and a token force of two warships, *Prince of Wales* and *Repulse.*

The report convinced Admiral Yamamoto that although an attack on Pearl Harbor was strategically illogical and extremely hazardous, the Japanese need no longer worry about British intervention. Armed with the information that the British had virtually written off Singapore, on 7th December 1941, without warning, the Japanese struck.

Japan had long intended a programme of expansion. In 1929 Count Tanaka, then Prime Minister, laid down what became Japan's *Mein Kampf.* 'Japan's food supplies and raw materials decrease in relation to her population. Our best policy,' he wrote, 'lies in expansion, first in China, then Malaya and India, Asia Minor and eventually Europe'. Though the Government was forced to disclaim this philosophy publicly, almost at once it set about implementing it, beginning with Manchuria in 1931, China in 1937 and French Indo-China in 1940.

The Japanese Army as a political force had gradually increased its power and, coming to Government in October 1941, saw the perfect opportunity to take on the West. This the army set about doing simultaneously against the United States at Pearl Harbor, and Britain in Malaya. Within days the Japanese were naval masters of the Pacific Ocean and within months they were shouldering the doors of India and Australia.

Such an attack had not been unforeseen. In the early 1930s the British Government decided that Japan had become so powerful, a counterweight was needed in the form of a great naval base at Singapore. This was finally completed in 1937. What General Dobbie discovered when he took over as GOC Malaya that same year was that the seemingly impregnable citadel of Singapore Island was only a stage fort - there was no back to it. But that was no cause for alarm said the strategists: the impassable jungles of Malaya would give sufficient protection.

But were the jungles impenetrable? Early in 1941 the Japanese had decided to find out. They set aside an area of Formosa, now Taiwan, to study jungle warfare and how it might be waged in Malaya: what tactics, clothing and equipment would be necessary; how the jungle could be penetrated and the rivers crossed. They discovered that the jungle could be an ally. Using a web of native paths it was possible to penetrate unseen to great depths. An engineering regiment attached to each division could throw up bridges over broad rivers - narrow ones could be spanned by planks laid on the backs of kneeling infantrymen. Food, medicine, clothing, arms and particularly the tactics of individual initiative were dictated by the confines of jungle warfare.

Plans for the invasion began to take shape, greatly assisted by an assiduous network of Japanese spies who had set up as barbers and photographers throughout Malaya in order to supply precise military information. From them the Japanese learned that Singapore lacked defences to the north, that the bulk of troops facing them would be Indian and that the British troops were mostly raw recruits sent to release experienced men for active theatres. They learned also that there was not a single tank among the enemy's armour. And perhaps most important, the Japanese learned that the British air force was composed mainly of obsolescent aircraft. Some of this information came from a New Zealand officer serving with the Indian Army on attachment to an air intelligence liaison unit. He was transmitting recognition codes to the Japanese air force which enabled them to approach without warning. His comrades noticed that he was never in the slit trenches during an air raid and suspicions were confirmed when he was found trying to hide a transmitting set which was still warm. Arrested, and just before the fall of Singapore, it is believed that he arrogantly told his captors that he would soon be a free man while they would all be dead or prisoners. The officer in charge drew his revolver and shot him dead.

General Percival DSO MC, the General Officer Commanding Malaya, with a fine First World War record, was a man of great personal courage, a hard-working and loyal subordinate, but excelling less in initiative than in staff work. He claimed even after the first bombs had fallen that to black out Singapore would be bad for civilian morale and there was nothing in the plans which required it. His defensive strength consisted of: the newly arrived capital ships *Prince of Wales* and *Repulse*; approximately 85,000 British and colonial troops, largely Indian, few of whom had combat service; 158 operational aircraft, mostly of an obsolescent type. There were no tanks.

Leading the invading armies was General Yamashita. At fifty-six and at the height of his army career, he was a master of the samurai code which demanded that a soldier carry out any task to the death. He was rigid, talented and ruthless, regarded by his subordinates as the finest general in the Japanese Army. Yet he was not popular with his superiors. He detested businessmen and politicians, believed the army should rule and that the war with the West was justified. Militarily he had done well in China and had been sent to Germany to study their methods. Offered five divisions for the invasion of Malaya, he replied that three would be sufficient. These three divisions consisted of 70,000 war-hardened combat troops supported by light and medium tanks, squadrons of Zero fighter planes which were the equal of British Hurricane fighters, and escorting naval vessels.

The pulsing drone of the enemy air fleets in the early morning skies was the first notice of war the authorities down on Singapore Island received. Then the bombs rained down on the brightly-lit town killing sixty-one civilians. Mid-morning, the British attempted a retaliatory raid on Singora with disastrous loss of planes which were no match for their Japanese opponents.

Meanwhile at Kota Bharu at the top of Malaya's east coast a Japanese seaborne invasion almost turned to disaster for the invaders when high seas and a determined defence by Dogras of the 8th Indian Infantry Brigade repulsed their initial efforts. But a false rumour that the airport was surrounded caused an order to retreat to be issued.

Further down the east coast Admiral Tom Phillips with his two great ships, the *Prince of Wales* and the *Repulse*, steamed north to catch the Japanese unawares. The aircraft carrier which should have accompanied them had unfortunately run aground at Jamaica. Without air cover, the ships were sitting ducks to the ace Japanese pilots in their torpedo bombers. Within an hour, in one of the worst disasters in British naval history, the Japanese torpedo bombers operating from Singora had sent both ships to the bottom with the loss of over 800 lives. Churchill later wrote that in all the war he had never received a more direct shock.

From then on the end was predictable. What was not predicted was the speed and efficiency of the Japanese advance or the ineffectiveness of the British command. Seldom in the history of war can there have been such a skein of muddle, confusion and stupidity: bridges blown on a rumour with half our forces on the wrong side of them; guns over-run while troops took shelter from the rain under trees; individual acts of heroism negated by a stream of orders to retreat and regroup.

And so, eight weeks after they had landed, the Japanese found themselves looking the several hundred yards across the straits at the Island of Singapore. In that time not one stick of defence had been raised to the north of the island. No air raid shelters had been constructed despite daily air raids. Lesser commanders found themselves surrounded by fantasy and frustration. Attempting to clear banana trees to improve his field of fire on the island within days of the end, a company commander was told he would require to get written permission. Another commander, trying to dig in on the golf course, was told by one of the club's committee that it was private property. Until the morning of surrender the Base Ordnance Depot was operating full regulation procedure of all paperwork in quadruplicate.

The end came quickly. The British had retreated to their 'impregnable' fortress and blown up the causeway behind them. On the 8th February the Japanese assault forces, numbering some 30,000, attacked, some in boats, some wading across the gap in the causeway, and some even swimming with their rifles on their backs. There followed a week of fierce fighting at the end of which the British forces had been driven back to the suburbs of Singapore City.

At Tanglin Military Hospital Japanese Imperial Guards burst into the wards, gunning down staff and bayoneting patients in the crowded corridors and on the operating tables.

The streets were crammed with a million refugees and legions of leaderless soldiers. The entire airforce was reduced to a total of four serviceable planes, one an old biplane. Piles of unburied dead from air raids littered the streets. The water supply which came mostly from the mainland had been cut. Great guns pointed uselessly out to sea. Singapore Island was a ring of fire as ruptured fuel storage tanks sent plumes of oily smoke to block out the sun, while ships, funeral pyres for a dying city, burned in the harbour.

On the afternoon of 15th February 1942 General Percival with a small escort of staff officers left his headquarters at Fort Canning carrying a large white flag and a Union Jack. He surrendered the garrison unconditionally to General Yamashita at his headquarters at the Ford Factory, Bukit Timah, some miles away. General Yamashita said afterwards that he would have liked to say a few words of solace to Percival but found this difficult through an interpreter. Eighty-five thousand troops laid down their arms to enter into three and a half years' captivity. Approximately a third of them did not survive.

The attack on Malaya was the Japanese Imperial Army's most brilliant campaign - an advance of 600 miles in fifty-four days at a cost of 10,000 casualties. Allied casualties, including surrendered troops, came to 38,496 British, 18,490 Australian, 67,340 Indian and 14,382 local volunteers.

The fall of Singapore marked virtually the end of Britain's imperial prestige. But it also marked virtually the high watermark of the Japanese thrust to Empire. Though they continued to gain territory, the tide was turning and afterwards in every theatre of war the Japanese were beaten back by superior troops until they collapsed in exhaustion and atom bomb trauma. At the end of the war, General Yamashita surrendered the Philippines to the Americans. Present at the official ceremony was General Percival, released from Prison Camp in Manchuria. Yamashita raised an eyebrow but otherwise remained impassive. A year later Yamashita was convicted of war crimes and was hanged.

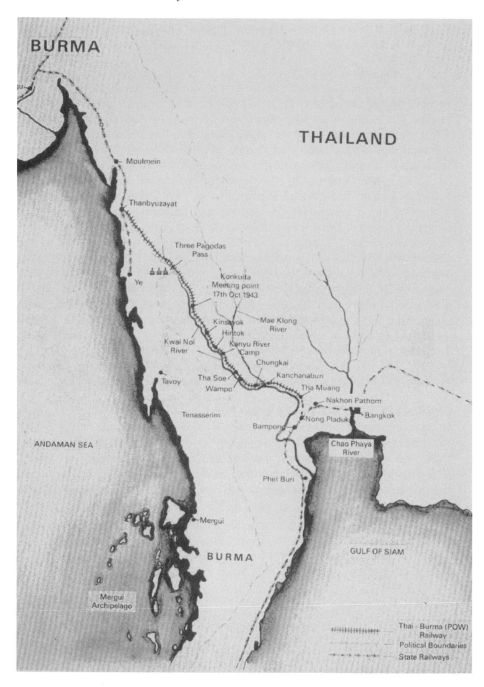

PART I
Fall of Empire

Singapore's Final Hours

ARGYLLS IN ACTION

Brigadier I A Stewart, Commanding Officer, 2nd Battalion Argyll &
Sutherland Highlanders

Brigadier Stewart's men, almost alone among British and Australian troops, had been trained by him in jungle warfare. At the end of the campaign he was ordered to escape to India from where the following report was broadcast on Bombay Radio.

On 14th December C Company was dispatched to the battle area on the Grik Road on the Siamese border. For four days they delayed the advance of at least three enemy battalions until the remainder of the Regiment was moved to that front. During this period they lost more than fifty per cent of their men. Tiger patrols were sent behind enemy lines. One had particular success in shooting up some staff carloads of Jap officers. Returning through a native village they were met by dreadful looking ruffians who yelled out, *'Weel, weel,* fancy meeting you here.' These were two Argyll scouts sent out some days before.

Rearguard action continued right down the length of Malaya, starting at the Siamese border where they had their first major battle and the first of their many successes. Fed-up waiting for the Japs to show, I decided to advance. As the bugler was about to sound, we received orders to retreat. The Japs tried a quick follow-up but were caught in a roadside ambush and their leading party was wiped out.

After that the Argylls had three goes at most successful rearguard fighting. One afternoon they were heavily engaged with an enemy battalion on the road frontally when another suddenly appeared approaching fast up the road behind them. Once the enemy got across the road the Argylls would be in trouble because it passed over a causeway which would be easy for the enemy to hold as a bottleneck. Our battalion watchwords were aggressiveness and speed and on this occasion they saved us. We dashed back on the attack and it succeeded. The enemy was thrown into confusion and lost a lot of men. The attack petered out and we got the whole battalion safely past the bottleneck.

One of our sections was watching a railway approach when a party of seventeen Japs, with more in the distance, walked down the railway and into the station. The Argyll officer ordered the armoured car in which he was travelling to fix the enemy frontally while he and his company sergeant major and his orderly attacked to the flank. They shot Japs right and left. When the Sergeant Major ran out of ammunition he took his tommy-gun by the barrel and clubbed several Japs over the head with it. It was only afterwards that he realised that his hands were badly burned by the barrel. The other men had got busy on the remaining Japs with their fists and finally with their tin hats. In all they killed fifteen. As the main Jap body was now approaching, the Argylls snatched up the least dead-looking Jap and beat a retreat.

It was in this battle that the Japs, having failed in both frontal and encircling attacks, brought tanks into action straight down the road. Three miles behind the Argylls was a thirty-yard broad river. It was a yellow fast-flowing flood and believed to be impassable. As there were no bridges, the scattered party of 120 found themselves faced with having to swim the flood if they wanted to get back. Several could not swim. In the growing darkness those Argylls on the south bank saw their mates coming down the north bank and great preparations for a rescue were made. They got hold of a long rope and one end of it was tied to an officer who then dived into the river. He came up looking very dazed indeed because the river was only four feet deep and he just about got concussion. So what might have been tragedy became comedy.

A further rearguard action to the Slim River saw the battalion's swansong. Until then they had never had a failure despite being continuously in action. At Slim, the Japs attacked straight down the road with thirty tanks - we had none. They scattered our troops into the jungle on either side and this time they were not able to get back. The Jap victory however cost them dear for the infantry were not able to follow up the success of the tanks.

On 29th January the Argylls moved back to do their last rearguard action at the causeway. They first piped their friends, the Gordons (92nd), over. Then, the last troops out of the mainland, the Argylls, came across, their pipes playing 'Highland Laddie' and 'Hundred Pipers'. And when I gave the word 'Blow!', up went seventy-five yards of the causeway in a colossal explosion.

THE DYING THROES

(Condensed)

J K Kerr, Royal Signals

Since our unit, No 6 Army Air Support Signals Squadron, no longer had a specific role because the Air Force had ceased to exist, a variety of jobs came our way. We found ourselves in the closing days of the battle for Singapore evacuated to a wooded area in the north west of the island which was under heavy attack by mortars. We were instructed to dig trenches in an open part of the camp to deposit therein our white sea kit bags which had to be set on fire - not a good sign.

As this was going on there filtered through the trees a number of Australian soldiers in a very unkempt state without arms or equipment. They started to rake through our kitbags and told us the Japs had captured their tucker wagon that morning 'so we just packed it in'.

A quick evacuation of our unit was ordered to the outskirts of Singapore. Our first job was to clear a bamboo hedge along the side of the road to provide a field of fire and a sergeant major placed us in rifle pits overlooking the road. He told us the Japanese army would be coming down the road shortly, and that there would be no retreat. We must fight to the last man. Of course I was scared but I was also angry that my young life was to end in a hole in the ground of an island thousands of miles away from Scotland.

However, the morning passed without incident and half of us were relieved for a meal. As we were finishing, a large American car drove up and out jumped an officer of the Military Police. Indicating about twelve of us, he said he was requisitioning us for a special job. We were bundled into the car. How we did it I do not know, but I remember I was standing on the near side running board with an arm hooked around the door pillar. So we set off screaming through Singapore streets with chaos all around and snipers taking pot-shots as we raced past.

At Keppel Harbour we were led to a godown where the officer told us our job was to stop Australians from deserting on to refugee ships and to shoot if necessary. (The Australians had fought well during the retreat but a small number of their leaderless troops had broken away). I thought to myself that this was a funny old war - I was fighting the Japanese this morning and now I was fighting Australians.

The first sight that greeted us was a Punjabi and an Australian having a blazing row over a carton of cigarettes. The Australian grabbed his rifle, put one up the spout and was about to fire until one of our group who had a Thomson sub-machine gun fired a burst into the water. The Military Police officer drew his revolver and ordered both soldiers back to their units. Some hope? There followed a frustrating and thankless task for the Australians were determined to get on to the *ss Empire Star* which was tied up to the dock. They climbed up the mooring ropes and anchor chain. They pushed their way up the gangway, elbowing aside women and children as well as wounded RAF. If we had attempted to use force to deny them access to the ship there would have been civilian casualties. In any case every few minutes we had to take cover as Japanese bombers and dive-bombers kept up a continuous bombardment.

Eventually the Captain of the *Empire Star* had enough and prepared to sail. As there were no dockers we had to take over and I found myself in charge of the stern mooring rope waiting to cast off. There were some Australians in the stern of the ship and they shouted 'C'mon Jock, climb up the rope. You are all dead men if you stay.' I said nothing and when the signal was given and the rope slackened I cast off the rope, allowing the ship to move from the dock. At that moment a burst of machine gunfire came from the stern of the ship and like one man we dropped to the ground. It was weird, for the ship's rail had been crowded with people laughing and waving, but when I looked again not a soul was to be seen. I presume the Australians thought we were all Military Police for whom they have an intense dislike.

The Military Police officer told us to pick one of the hundreds of abandoned vehicles and make our own way back to our unit. Though we did not know the way, we set off into the hell that was Singapore town where everything seemed to be burning and all around the sky was obliterated by swirling black clouds. There was an ominous quietness as we drove north. When an Indian patrol, which, judging by the blood stained bandages, had recently been in action stopped us and told us that the Japs were just ahead, we turned the vehicle round and went back to the docks where we found that a large RAF unit had taken over. Charlie my mate, ever resourceful, had picked up a RAF cap which he placed on his head and we were waved through and told to join their regimental police.

Around 3 am, a ghostly grey shape appeared out of the darkness - a ship! It was the *ss Kedah*, a coastal vessel, and it stopped by the simple expedient of crashing into the pier. I was given the job of guarding the gangplank but this time there was no disorderly crush. I was then approached by an army major who said I looked like a good soldier. Would I volunteer for a suicide squad which was going back into the jungle to harass the Japs? I apologised and pleaded a previous engagement! When all the RAF were aboard, the Provost Marshall came along and told us to come aboard. This we did with alacrity.

Shortly after sailing we came under attack from Japanese dive-bombers. We gave a good account of ourselves with small arms and they sheered off, leaving us to the mercy of the high level bombers.

When I was ordered to the bridge to assist the naval signaller I had a grandstand view of the ensuing battle. The *Kedah* was part of a convoy which included the *Empire Star* and the Australian cruiser *HMAS Durban*. For the next four hours we were bombed continuously and both the *Empire Star* and the *Durban* were hit. We escaped, thanks to the seamanship of our captain who watched the fall of the bombs, and having taken over the helm evaded all the attacks. But just in case, I loosened my bootlaces, and, sharks or not, prepared if necessary, even though I could not swim, to try and make one of the nearby islands. I will always remember dealing with a message from *ss Ipoh* which said she could not keep up with the speed of the convoy and was therefore proceeding at her own pace. It was sad to see her dropping back in the far distance with Jap planes still buzzing about but I am glad to say that I heard later that she, like ourselves, had made it to Batavia in Java.

The next three or four weeks were chaotic as no one knew what was happening. We spent our time in Batavia at the local cinema and the Micky Mouse Nightclub. The native women were incredible and each one seemed to be offering her charms without reserve. The local word for it was *'mak mak'*.

This of course could not last. The Japs eventually landed in Batavia and we were once again on active service but after a week or so the Dutch capitulated and there was no alternative but to hurriedly withdraw. There was a rumour that there was to be a Dunkirk-type evacuation at a place called Tjiliatjap on the south coast of Java. A nightmare journey in a commandeered vehicle and we joined the convoy which had somehow to hide during the day. When we reached the mountains however the road deteriorated to little more than a dirt track along sheer cliffs. I heard that one of the trucks went over the edge leaving no hope of survivors. Eventually the road disappeared altogether into the jungle. We decided to press on to reach the south coast. The first thing we met was an armoured car with a military policeman sitting on the bonnet and beside a box full of silver Dutch guilders - it looked like the whole of the Javanese treasury. He tried to persuade us to fill our pockets, but what was the use? The next hazard was a burning Bren gun carrier with ammunition exploding in all directions.

We reached a clearing with what had been a paddy-field and four of our group argued that they should go over the top to see if they could get some food. The four disappeared over the top and as a few minutes later we heard several bursts of machine gun fire, there was no doubt of their fate. We turned back and eventually came on a road with a convoy of vehicles. One was a 15 cwt truck. I jumped on the tailboard. The convoy turned off the road into a yard where we were ordered to dismount.

My lift had been right into a prison camp.

ESCAPE FROM SINGAPORE
Captain J K Crerar, Edinburgh

On the 15th February 1942 when Singapore fell, the remains of two batteries of the 1st Indian Heavy AA Regiment were stationed in a police station near Raffles Hotel. After carrying out the cease-fire terms, Captain Charles Baillie, 2nd Lieutenants Dick Seymour, Ray Watson and myself, decided we would try to reach Sumatra. We collected our water bottles and some food, and after searching for three hours we rescued a small sampan from the burning docks.

We set off paddling fast on a south-westerly course knowing that our chances of reaching cover were pretty slim. It was only two and a half hours until the dawn when luckily we sighted a small island. We were still only a few miles from Singapore and could see the many fires very clearly. As we drew near the tiny island, the sea took hold of our small craft. Before we knew what was happening, the sampan was dashed against the rocky shore. All our stores and equipment were lost and the boat was holed.

After a long struggle we managed to beach it, and exhausted, crawled into the undergrowth and soon fell asleep. The sun was overhead when I awoke. I was very thirsty and was leaving to look for water when I heard men's voices just below me. I woke up Charles Baillie and we decided to remain under cover in case they were Japs. After about ten minutes we heard someone approaching. The undergrowth parted and much to our relief some Chinese appeared carrying a mug of water and biscuits. They beckoned us to follow them to their huts. We gathered from signs that they had seen us landing and had rescued and repaired our sampan which had drifted out to sea and they had also fitted a small sail.

During the day we were given coffee and tinned sardines from their meagre rations. They also told us to make for an island we could see to the south-west. We left some money in one of the huts for them as they would not accept any payment for the goods they had given us.

The four of us continued our journey as dusk was falling. We had three miles of open sea to cross and the wind was blowing strongly. After two exciting hours we finally reached calmer water where a strong current took us along at such a good speed that we passed the island we were making for. We drifted on and when dawn was breaking we found ourselves lost in a mangrove swamp which we at first thought to be land. It took a great deal of time and difficulty to find our way out. It was broad daylight when at last we left the swamp and quickly paddled to another island close at hand.

We soon found a friendly village. Small Malay boys climbed trees and threw down coconuts. Others brought curried rice, fruit and coffee and after feeding well we fell asleep under the palm trees. We had decided to travel at night only as there was a danger of Japanese planes spotting us. All day long we heard their familiar drone. During that afternoon, however, two Malay villagers said they would take us to a Dutch island where they knew a large ship was evacuating the European population. We accepted the offer. For protection in case we were spotted by the Japs, they built a small covering over part of their boat. This we hid under as soon as we heard a plane.

After many weary hours we eventually arrived at the Dutch island only to find that the ship had gone some hours before. We said goodbye to our two Malay friends who departed immediately for their village. After a good sleep in a deserted hut, along with some other British and Australians, we contacted the headman of a large village. To our amazement he produced a map showing a route to Sumatra via a neighbouring island only a mile distant. Before Singapore fell, this route had apparently been organised by our Intelligence in case of an evacuation. The headman arranged to ferry all of us to the island. He also told us that a motor launch made regular trips from there to Sumatra. On the island we found large dumps of food, water and medical supplies. At this time, divided into numerous parties, there were about forty men. Among them I met Findlay Cessford, a Lieutenant in the HKSRA, who accompanied me in the latter part of my journey to Ceylon. As Charles Baillie was Senior Officer, he decided that each party would draw rations daily and that lookouts would be posted. This done, all we had to do was to sit and wait for the launch.

Forty-eight hours passed without any sign of her, but eventually a junk dropped anchor and a handful of men came ashore. To our surprise a Gunner Lieutenant was in charge. Miraculously, he had brought the remains of his troop all the way from Singapore, and on calling at some island for food, had been directed to this food dump. The Lieutenant said he had over a hundred men on board including a number of Australians he had picked up on the way. He agreed to take everyone on the island provided it was understood that he was skipper. All arms had to be handed over to his quartermaster who would be responsible for rations. According to the map, the next food dump was at the mouth of the Indragiri River in Sumatra, eighty miles distant, which we estimated would be two days sailing. How wrong we were!

It was a relief to be aboard the junk and out of range of the mosquitoes and flies. The boat was about one hundred tons and powered by one large sail. However, there was little wind and we lay helpless in the calm. After spending a night in the same position, the ship at last began to move. With the help of long oars we finally punted the junk into deeper water, and a slight wind began to move us along.

It was again dark when, travelling in a south-westerly direction, we eventually entered the Malacca Straits. The wind rose steadily during the night and we began to make fast progress. I was below deck in the large hold and was trying to sleep when I felt a dull thud. There was a lot of shouting and when I came on deck I found the junk had run aground. In the darkness I could see the shadow of land close by. It was soon light enough to see we had hit a hidden sandbank about a mile to the north west of Sumatra. There was nothing but thick jungle and no sign of life. We must have run aground about high tide, for it was twenty-four hours before we pushed the junk clear.

This delay had upset our calculations and rations were immediately reduced to two bowlfuls of rice and one pint of water per day. We headed south-east along the coast for three days, making poor progress owing to an unfavourable wind. One morning someone spo ted two dots on the horizon which we soon realised were heading in our direction. Our skipper immediately ordered the arms to be issued. Everyone was ordered below except a few, including myself, who were to act as a Chinese crew. Some of us wore coolie hats. Soon we made the vessels out to be fast motor boats which must have been Japanese. Our disguise must have been good, and we were very pleased when, only a few miles off, they changed course to a northerly direction, and were soon speeding away from us.

Our food and water position was becoming desperate when at last we rounded the headland and changed course to the west. Another day's sailing brought us to the mouth of the great Indragiri river. However, our troubles were not yet over. There was no sign of a food dump or for that matter any habitation, only jungle which lined both banks of the river. As the Indragiri is tidal we made little or no progress for another day. Suddenly, round a bend appeared a motor boat coming our way. It was manned by a Royal Scot Lieutenant who had been making regular trips to the island which we had left about a week ago. He took the junk in tow and towed it a few miles up river to a village. Charles Baillie, Dick Seymour, Ray Watson, Findlay Cessford and myself went ashore. Findlay's fountain pen, our only possession, was exchanged for pineapples which we ate greedily.

We left the village that evening for Ringat, several miles up river, with the motor boat towing the junk which now had about 200 men aboard. Next morning we had reached a point fifteen miles from Ringat when the junk again ran aground. As the motor boats could not pull us off they left to try and find additional help. The skipper told us that we could go ashore and walk or else remain on board. The five of us went into consultation and Findlay Cessford and myself decided to walk. We were joined ashore by two gunners and it so happened that we were the only men on the junk to reach safety.

The fifteen miles to Ringat appeared ten times as long. The sun beat down on our uncovered heads. One of the gunners who had no shoes tied banana leaves round his feet to protect them from the stony path. We reached Ringat in a little over four hours, where, on arrival, the launch took us to a hospital. The many sores which had broken out over our bodies were treated and after a good meal we were driven thirty miles to a transit camp.

The transit camp was in the factory of a rubber estate and was under the command of a British Colonel who had a Captain as his adjutant. On arrival, each officer was given a number of men to look after. My men were survivors from *HMS Prince of Wales*. Findlay Cessford was in charge of another group including the two gunners who had made the march with us. Each group was given some duty to perform. Just when we had completed a full day's cookhouse duty the CO asked if my section would continue for another twelve hours as another large intake was expected in the early hours of the following morning. Findlay Cessford was more fortunate: he left that evening for the next camp.

During that night, in heavy rain, my section was busy cooking and serving meals. The new arrivals included Charles Baillie, Dick Seymour and Ray Watson. The following day my party left by bus for the next camp and in saying goodbye to my friends I little thought it would be for the last time.

As it happened our bus was the last to leave the camp in the rubber estate. We started off on a 300-mile journey along a good road, which however, soon turned into a mere track. The bus driver was an Indonesian who possessed an endearing grin, but could not speak a word of English. We travelled up and down mountains and over many large rivers. Once we met Dutch troops who were on their way to repel a Japanese force which had made a landing to the north. After fifteen hours of being jostled about and completely in the hands of our driver, we arrived at the next stopping place. It was a pleasant town, high up in the mountains. I was billeted in the hotel and enjoyed the luxury of a bath and clean sheets on a soft bed. Findlay Cessford had already arrived and looked quite different without his beard.

The next day I went to hospital as my legs were badly swollen and was advised to stay in bed for a day or two. I decided to carry on, and the next night we travelled ninety miles to Padang on the south-west coast. We arrived at the port in the early hours of the morning. Later in the day we were given some money by the Dutch military authorities. I bought a shirt, stockings, towel, soap and toothbrush. We were billeted in a school and on arriving back from the shopping expedition we were told that we would embark that night. Sure enough, as darkness fell we entered the dock during an air raid and were soon safely aboard. The Dutch ship sailed in the early morning for Batavia, but when the Captain heard that Java had fallen, he changed course for Colombo which we reached in eight days.

I owed much to the many people who helped me on my way: the Chinese and Malays; the unknown Gunner Lieutenant who commanded the junk; the Royal Scot Lieutenant who towed the junk up the Indragiri River; the CO and adjutant of the transit camp in the rubber estate who by their sense of duty decided quite voluntarily to stay behind to organise the escape route; and lastly, Charles Baillie, Findlay Cessford, Dick Seymour and Ray Watson, who made the whole journey possible.

Selarang Barrack Square, Changi, 1ˢᵗ - 5ᵗʰ September 1942

The Japanese troops who captured Singapore cannot have expected 80,000 POWs to deal with. The British and Australians were therefore herded into the large cantonment area of Changi, fenced off, and left largely to their own devices. In the course of time, however, the Japanese planned the large-scale employment of the prisoners on works of military importance (totally contrary to international rules of war), and as a preliminary step, on 31ˢᵗ August 1942 required all POWs to sign forms promising not to escape. When all but a few 'odd bods' refused, the order was given for all POWs, except those in hospital, to move into Selarang Barracks, producing the extraordinary scene shown in the sketch. There were only two stand-pipes to supply water, no sewage facilities, and field and machine-guns were posted at the corners of the square. The digging of latrine-trenches was started at once, and continued throughout the four-and-a-half days there. Food was confined to rice and anything the POWs had been able to bring in.

The senior Lieutenant Colonel present was Col E B Holmes, Manchester Regiment. For substantial periods each day he stood to attention in front of a table at which Japanese officers sat. A small, well turned-out figure, he refused the offer of a chair, and plainly, in sight of all the POWs, was holding out against the Japanese. On 4th September he ordered all POWs to sign, and later, in a clear and explicit written order, explained that the Japanese had stated that if we did not sign at once, all hospital patients would be moved to the square. He had been advised by the Medical Officers that about 200 would be likely to die through being moved, and that others included carriers of infections and contagions which would spread like wildfire. He explained that our signing was strictly 'under duress' and that he would report the circumstances in full to HM Government and take responsibility for the signing.

Before this incident morale among the troops had been faltering badly. There had been a general reaction against well-meaning attempts to restore morale (which had been severely affected by the exhaustion of the campaign and the shock of defeat, compounded by poor communication with the troops). Colonel Holmes's conduct, the first visible example of resistance to the Japanese, had an immediate effect in raising morale. Shortly after our release from Selarang on 5th September, the dispatch of working parties to Thailand and other destinations was speeded-up, and the benefit from Colonel Holmes's conduct was seen in better morale and better relations between officers and men. - Drawing by G S Gimson from the original which had been lent to him.

CHANGI JAIL DITTY
J L Woods

When orders were issued in Singapore
For nationals then in a state of war
With Japan to parade in the morning
For internment behind the bars,
We were told, 'You'll parade in the clothes you wear
With a shirt and a pair of socks to spare,
And be ready to ride on shanks' mare,'
So I said good-bye to my cars!

The following day was a nasty rub
When we turned up in front of the Cricket Club
Which no longer resembled a friendly pub
And hope seemed very remote.
And we hung around till the midday sun
Decided he'd have a spot of fun,
And when I got really well 'on the run'
Well I bade good-bye to my coat!

We marched away to a prison cell
And found the conditions simple - well
I wasn't surprised at the kind of smell
When I saw the kind of dirt.
My first experiments proved that I
Could with very much greater success apply
The soap to myself than my collar and tie
So l said good-bye to my shirt!

I'm a married man but I never knew
The dozens of things that housewives do
To pull their unfortunate husbands through
And spare them unpleasant shocks.
So when I found that my toes were bare
And that even the most expensive wear
In hosiery cannot do self-repair
Well! I said good-bye to my socks!

I wasn't the only one to find
The life we had known had been left behind,
And some of my friends were sufficiently kind
To hint I was overdressed.
And being a friendly sort of bloke
Who dislikes being different from other folk,
Of course I could only answer 'Oke,'
And I said good-bye to my vest!

I very soon came to realise
That everything flourishes once - and dies,
And when you begin to run out of supplies
It is no good getting the blues.
The leather that used to protect my toe
Had done all its flourishing years ago,
And it started to oscillate to and fro
So I said good-bye to my shoes!

Now it isn't for me to create a fuss
About all sorts of things that had happened to us,
But I couldn't forget a man misses the bus
If he starts to plough and recants.
So I squared my shoulders and braced my knees,
And converted my hanky into 'V's,
And in spite of a somewhat chilly breeze
I said good-bye to my pants!

Now a lady might think that was going too far,
But it still spoilt the ship for a ha'p'orth of tar,
And when RAPWI arrived at the harbour bar
To conduct us over the seas,
I found that they wouldn't allow me afloat
Till with tears in my eyes and a lump in my throat
I succeeded but barely in catching the boat
By saying good-bye to my 'V's.

SNAPSHOT

On Thursday 12th February over a million refugees crammed on to Singapore Island including civilian women and children. Victims of the official pronouncement that Singapore was an impregnable fortress, many had refused previous offers of evacuation. Amid the inferno of burning oil tanks, the choking smell of burning rubber, swirling blankets of tarry fog, scything shrapnel and low-level aerial gunning, they frantically waved their paper passes at soldiers. But the Japanese had vowed to prevent another Dunkirk and a battle fleet awaited the evacuees. Fifty-two ships sailed that night for Java: forty-eight went to the bottom or were stranded on islands where their passengers and crew starved to death or were captured. A group of military nurses, wading ashore from their bombed ship, were machine-gunned to death in the surf.

PART II
POW Camps

Kanyu Camp, River Kwai, 14th March 1943

A typical riverside camp with huts of bamboo frames and attap (palm-leaf thatch) roofs, with a low roof-ridge. Sleeping-platforms of split-bamboo ran the full length of each side of the hut and generally allowed each man a two-feet wide sleeping space – his 'home' for the duration. The huts deteriorated rapidly, especially after the monsoon rains began. - G S Gimson

FOUR GEORGE CROSSES FOR HONG KONG

John R Harris, The Royal Engineers

In March 1943 I was a member of a truck unloading party when a lorry arrived with a load of wood for the cookhouse. As it was being unloaded I moved to the front of the truck where the Chinese driver sat in his cab. Standing by him was a Japanese guard and eight others were twenty feet away. Just as the last log was removed the driver gave a warning cough and threw out an old cigarette packet. I picked it up with the sweepings of bark off the floor of the truck. My heart was thumping as I carried the packet into the latrines, but it had nothing in it. I took the packet with some disappointment to a very outstanding man, Colonel L A Newnham. He fetched a piece of charcoal from the cookhouse and held the paper up to the heat. Immediately a message became visible. Our excitement was intense and I was struck by the extreme bravery of the Chinese driver for he had no idea who I was. His trust had to be absolute. I was given a reply which was hidden in a cigarette packet by Colonel Newnham. It was left in the truck when the same driver was next on duty.

For the first few days I dealt with the messages on my own. The risk in replying to them was considerable. Newnham brought in Captain G V Bird, who was, like myself, both an officer in the Royal Engineers and an architect. Through Newnham's drive, messages both in and out increased to almost one a day. When suspicion was being aroused as to why Godfrey Bird or myself attended the unloading of every supply truck, Colonel Newnham decided that each POW hut should have one officer to pass the messages. Nine more officers were therefore told about BAAG (British Army Aid Group).

The concealment of messages became more and more sophisticated with the use of rubber bands so that small packets could be fixed to the underside of the vehicle.

The messages from Argyle Street, the officers' POW camp, contained not only the names of those who were alive in the camp and plans for escape, but also information relating to defences, the results of American bombing, the movement of Japanese shipping and aircraft at Hong Kong. and information on the Indian National Army. This information was used by the Allies and the US Air Force in particular.

As the weeks passed the risks of smuggling messages became greater. One of the eleven officers involved, Lieutenant Ralph Goodwin of the Royal New Zealand Naval Volunteer Reserve therefore invented the 'bolt'. He fashioned it in wood, exactly copying the steel bolt used in the construction of the frame of the supply lorry. The bolt was passed to BAAG members outside the camp who adjusted the supply lorry to take it. Messages and drugs were hidden within the hollow bolt. The officer on duty would remove the false bolt from the lorry and insert a new one with a message. Once practised this took only a few seconds. At the height of this activity Newnham's messages took four to seven days to reach India through China.

Newnham gathered information from many sources, not least from Captain J L Flynn of the 2nd/14th Punjab Regiment. He was in touch with loyal Indians who were in a POW camp adjoining Argyle Street. They had already established their own intelligence system through other Indians who were working for the Japanese. In mid-June 1943, the Chinese driver, Hung Hoi, reported that Lee, the original driver, had been arrested. Then on 1st July we realised that Hung Hoi was acting under Japanese orders.

It was too late. The Japanese had infiltrated the BAAG system in Hong Kong. The next day Flight Lieutenant H B Gray, Sergeant R J Ruttledge and Sergeant R J Hardy from Shamshuipo were arrested as well as Lieutenant I R Haddock from our group in Argyle Street. The two leaders, Captain Ford in Shamshuipo and Colonel Newnham in Argyle Street, were arrested ten days later. Mass arrests were next made at Stanley Internment Camp where security was poor. At the Indian camp Captain M A Apsari, the mainstay of the Indian resistance, was also arrested.

In October 1943, thirty-two British internees from Stanley, together with Chinese civilians and Captain Apsari were tried by the Japanese. The charge was espionage though all they had done was listen to the wireless sets. The brief trial was a complete mockery of justice. The President, Lieutenant Colonel Fujimoto, at one stage slept for half an hour before smoking in the corridor outside. The accused were given virtually no opportunity to defend themselves. They were sentenced to death by decapitation. The affair was cruel and bloody with some executions so inept that lives were ended by shooting.

On 1st December 1943 six POW servicemen were tried: Newnham; Ford; Gray; Haddock; and Sergeants Hardy and Ruttledge. The Japanese charged them with receiving messages from BAAG and smuggling fifteen messages to BAAG. The Japanese did not try to prove that the information passed was of military significance, although it was. The officers were sentenced to death and the NCOs to fifteen years. The officers had been continuously and terribly tortured during their imprisonment, but refused to betray their comrades. At the end only Captain Ford could walk. They were shot on the 18th December 1943.

After the arrests Major C K Boxer called a meeting of the small group in Argyle Street camp of those of us 'in the know' who were left. Most volunteered to continue but BAAG made no further approaches. Their organisation in Hong Kong had collapsed.

After the war King George VI approved the posthumous awards of a Victoria Cross to Company Sergeant Osborne for his attack on Mount Butler, a George Cross to Mr John Alexander Fraser for his action of extreme bravery in Stanley, and no fewer than four George Crosses to: Colonel A Newnham, The Middlesex Regiment; Captain Douglas Ford, The Royal Scots; Flight Lieutenant H B Gray, Royal Air Force; Captain M A Ansari, 5/Rajputs.

In all 152 George Crosses were awarded between 1940 and 1985. I think it should be more widely known that Hong Kong has been the only place, as far as I can find out, where four George Crosses were awarded for the same event. By their gallantry these officers saved the lives of their comrades who had worked with them and shared their dangers. There was no inspiration from the heat of battle to sustain them: only superhuman effort of control over months in the cold of the torture chamber. These men remained silent and refused to implicate fellow prisoners and friends. They should be remembered.

MORE MEMORIES OF ARGYLE STREET

Lieutenant Colonel A J N Warrack, MBE

As a former inmate and Medical Officer of Argyle Street POW Camp, Hong Kong, from 1942 to 1944 I can add to 'Four George Crosses for Hong Kong' as the late Godfrey Bird was, I am proud to say, a particular friend of mine. In Hut 10, Argyle Street, we ate in small groups or messes of five or six officers. My group consisted of Hector Harland, Royal Scots, who was Brigade Major, Hong Kong Infantry Brigade, Peter Belton who was Staff Captain, two other friends and Godfrey Bird. It is possible that one or two of us in the summer of 1943 suspected that something mysterious was going on. The late Peter Belton, I recall, encouraged us to make up small parcels of tinned Red Cross food 'in case we were moved'. However I had no idea that Godfrey Bird was involved in any way.

Another thing that made me wonder what was going on was when General Maltby, our General Officer Commanding, took me, a mere Captain, for strolls around the huts asking me how far our sick would be able to walk in case of 'a sudden move'. Then in late June or July 1943 Colonel Newnham came into my little consulting room with a slip of paper in his hand saying, 'Doctor, Doctor have you any iodine?' He dabbed the iodine on the note and said, 'My God, we've been betrayed' or words to that effect. 'I'm for it.' Guessing that something odd was happening, I gave him an injection of vitamins which, rather luckily, I happened to have. Sure enough, the following day Colonel Newnham was taken out. Godfrey Bird, like all of us, was upset but gave no indication that he was in any way involved.

Nearly a year later, about June 1944, many of us were taken out of Argyle Street and sent to Japan where I spent the last year of the war working at Shinagow 'Hospital' Camp in Tokyo Bay. The greatest excitement we had there was the bombing, and being set on fire by our American allies!

As far as I know, Argyle Street was closed and occupants moved to Shamshuipo soon after I left. I certainly remember saying goodbye to Godfrey Bird at that time. Now whether he was given away by carrying on his involvement in Shamshuipo, or whether the Japanese were rather cunning and hoped they might find out something more by allowing him to continue, I do not know. Godfrey survived torture and imprisonment and was awarded the George Medal. He later continued his architectural career in industry for many years. As well as the four George Crosses therefore, there was the George Medal.

Much of the involvement of the British Army Aid Group is well documented in the book *'At The Going Down of the Sun'* by Oliver Lindsay, the Grenadier who took and still takes a great interest in the history of the Hong Kong war. The book was published by Hamish Hamilton Ltd in 1981.

SNAPSHOT

One of the first jobs prisoners on Singapore Island had was clearing up the bombed docks where some of the warehouses were stacked with food, not all of which got to its destination in Jap ration dumps. The Jap sergeant in charge of a working party could not catch the prisoners at it, but had a pretty good idea of how it was done. 'I show you,' he told his party of 'diggers'. He picked up a box of tinned fish and carried it towards a lorry. The prisoners watched with interest. Part way there he appeared to tire and laid the box on the ground. Looking round quickly, he took a tin from the box and slipped it under his hat on the ground. Then he carried the box to the lorry. Returning in triumph, he said, 'I very good understand.' Then he picked up his hat with a flourish - the tin of fish had vanished.

Chungkai Camp Hospital: Skin Wards

Chungkai was a vast camp, in effect, a base hospital. There were ultimately more than 12,000 men there, nearly all of whom would, in civilised conditions, have been in hospital. Many of the men were suffering from tropical diseases or the results of severe malnutrition, overwork and brutality. Skin diseases were endemic. Hospital equipment was almost entirely lacking apart from makeshift substitutes. In the foreground of this sketch a man is being treated for septic scabies (almost universal) with sulphur. Note the wooden 'washbasin' and 'bedpan'. - G S Gimson

WAS IT BUSHIDO?

William Dennenberg

A photograph featuring a row of Australian prisoners in the process of being decapitated inspired William Dennenberg to write 'Was it Bushido?' Perhaps these prisoners were the lucky ones? In later years, as reports of officially sanctioned sadism entered the public domain, he learned they had indeed suffered a much less painful death than many thousands of others. So much of the cruelty, excused as Bushido (the Japanese code of honour), was driven by a compulsive, addictive urge for pleasure.

O, fortunate man:
Wrists bound, knees bent, head bowed,
Staring into the shadowed trench;
The blade is swift, the slice is sure.
Sightless, he sees what might have been.
Crushed into a basket, the wicker constrains
The drowning man's despairing, hopeful struggle,
While the clear salt water scalds his lungs.
Or, Trailed behind the boat as shark bait,
Leaking blood to attract the sport
And excite the laughter.

Perhaps, at dusk,
Strung by his thumbs to a branch,
(His toes, even with the rocks attached,
Yet still failing to reach the ground)
He awaits the morning's bayonet drill.
His friends had had it worse. Old Joe,
Trussed with barbed wire, mouth stopped,
Pumped through his nose with water,
Died beneath the boots that jumped and split
His distended stomach open
To their wearers' laughter.

But the destruction of the body is nothing.
The ritual is spiritual. They do it for the pain;
And, yet better, for the agony,
And for the ecstasy the agony gives them.
O, how they love their cruelty,
These little yellow men.

Thank God: he hadn't been a woman,
A pleasured nurse, gang-raped through the long night hours,
Tortured near to death,
Taken to the beach to wash
Irremediable stains
From broken body,
And machine-gunned standing in the waves.
Or, disembowelled to win a bet:
The soldier won (it was a boy);
The woman lost (the child, her life)
As God's blood dripped into the gutter.

And now, in the last few seconds of a lifetime,
Deep inside that shadowed trench
He sees his children playing in the sand,
Their mother, mourning, watching.
The blessed engraved blade sings its dirge:
The blood spurts, mushrooms,
Driven by the final heartbeat.

The trench is black.
His head falls into the abyss.

LOCKED IN A LAVATORY
Ian MacKenzie, Gargunnoch

Escaping was something I never considered for two reasons. Firstly, there was no place to go when you got outside, though getting outside was relatively simple for this was certainly no Colditz. Secondly, if caught, it meant instant execution. Two Gordon Highlanders attempted to escape from Changi which was really rather foolhardy. They were caught on the beach trying to get hold of a boat. One was executed by sword on the spot and the other made a run for it. He sustained a bad sword slash across the shoulder but did make it back to Changi where he was hidden away until the wound had healed.

At one time I shared a corner of one of the rooms with Corporal Hepburn, Gordon Highlanders. It so happened that Wee Heppie had a Chinese girlfriend who lived about three or four miles from our camp. He wanted to visit her and insisted that I accompany him. On reflection, I suppose it was rather silly but there were very few Japs about. For a part of the way we kept to the undergrowth and to the quiet roads. We finally arrived at Wee Heppie's girlfriend's place of residence. As we peered out from the undergrowth just across the road we could see a Jap staff car duly bedecked with a pennant parked right outside the house. From this we deduced that the young lady was otherwise engaged and that the only thing we could do was retrace our steps.

We reached a point about half a mile from camp. As we walked along a quiet road two Japanese soldiers suddenly came round the bend of the road on bikes. It was too late to dive into the undergrowth so we thought the best thing we could do was to bluff it out as if we were supposed to be there and to give them a smart salute. Unfortunately this did not work and they took us along to the *Kempi,* the Japanese military police headquarters, in Orchard Road.

As the *Kempi* had a reputation that would make the Gestapo look like a group of Sunday school teachers, we were very concerned. They locked us up in a tennis court and mounted a machine gun outside the fence. I suppose when it was increasingly evident that we were not attempting to escape and were in fact making our way back, the Japanese dealt with us leniently by their standards and sentenced us to fourteen days in the 'No Good House'. This was to prove to be a masterpiece of understatement for Wee Heppie and I were locked in a very small lavatory and fed on rice and water once a day. It was a very small lavatory, just enough room for the pedestal and one person and no window - just a small grill very high up.

During the fourteen days we were not allowed out. I can still remember the utter boredom and the hunger but was thankful to be alive.

Towards the end of our period of incarceration we were both pretty weak. Heppie kept being sick and had great difficulty in keeping the rice down. At the end of our time, we were let out and duly went back to work, like model prisoners that we were!

I just do not know what happened to Heppie. I do not even know whether he survived the three and a half years in prison camp.

SNAPSHOT

Around us lay a thousand miles of ocean. Behind us lay a thousand miles of jungle. Escape, except immediately after surrender, was impossible. Yet one or two did try. In May, Q Branch, which was compiling a secret list of atrocities, asked me to interview one of our chaps who had made it to the mainland and got halfway up the peninsula before being caught. He said he had been paraded daily before a firing squad only to be marched back to his cell. Later, he was handed over to a Sikh unit which had defected. They put his head in a vice to try to find out how he had managed to get over to the mainland. Then he was brought back to camp. A fortnight later he was taken to the beach with three other POWs and before several hundred of us, was confronted by a Sikh firing squad. The Sikhs were nervous: they missed the fatal shot. Pointing to his heart he cried out, 'Hit me here.'

A CHILD IN CHINA

Moira Barbour, Aberdeen

This is the first time I have ever written about my experiences as a child so many years ago. People say that your childhood forms you. If this is true then I am today what happened to me over fifty years ago. Even today I can close my eyes and recall events which happened then and re-live them all again, sometimes with fear, sometimes with laughter and sometimes with sadness.

Going back in time to 1942, I lived with my parents and younger sister in Shanghai, China. I had a very idyllic childhood with all the comforts and privileges of a child of a western country living in the Far East in the thirties and early forties. I was eight years old in December 1941 when the Japanese bombed Pearl Harbor and for over a year until February 1943 when we were interned, we lived as a family not knowing what was going to happen to us. I remember quite clearly the tense atmosphere, the restriction on liberty, the curfews imposed on us by the Japanese, and on my enquiring why everyone was always talking about the war and the Japanese, my parents would tell me not to worry. Children sense atmospheres very acutely and during that period, I certainly did.

In February 1943 the Japanese soldiers came to our apartment and took us in trucks to our first camp which had been a school. I remember we were allocated a room for the four of us. We had been allowed to take our beds, and what we could carry, and the room held just that. From then on each day we had roll calls and had to stand outside our rooms and be counted. I remember how frightened I was as the Japanese guards always approached us with their swords dangling at their sides. In the two and a half years we were interned, I never got over the fear of those roll calls as the Japanese guards were so unpredictable and the least little annoyance would start them off shouting, pushing and hitting, especially if they were drunk. Even to this very day, if I see a war film with Japanese soldiers, this fear comes flooding back to me.

Life settled into a routine. With only a very few showers and toilets for over 1,500 people, times for use were allocated. The men in the camp had various chores to perform. Children were more or less left to their own devices until some sort of schooling was arranged with the help of a few teachers in our camp. We had an hour or so at school per day and after that we could do what we wanted. As far as the children were concerned, it was just a time for playing and getting into mischief as all children do. It is amazing how any child can adapt to a strange situation.

My most vivid memory is of being hungry all the time: waking up in the morning hungry and going to bed at night hungry. The food we got consisted mostly of rice and maize and if we were lucky, some fish. During the years we were interned we received three Red Cross parcels. We were supposed to receive one each a month and after the war ended, piles of parcels, reaching practically to the ceiling, were discovered in a warehouse. As a result of my always being so hungry during this period of my life I hate wasting food. When the war ended I was nearly twelve years of age and weighed approximately fifty-nine pounds.

During the first few months of being interned we had a Japanese Commandant who had been educated in Britain and was quite sympathetic and lenient towards the children. If they required dental treatment, for example, they were allowed out of camp with a parent to receive treatment. On one occasion I had to attend the dentist. He was going to pull a tooth out as I had an abscess. He was not going to give me an injection before pulling my tooth but when my mother made a special request for one on the grounds that I was only a child, he reluctantly agreed. I would not sit still in the chair as, not only was I in pain, but I was very frightened, and I remember him hitting me. To this day I am very frightened of going to the dentist. The medical situation was very bad because if you fell ill there were no medicines though from time to time the Japanese would give us injections for cholera, typhoid and other diseases. On these occasions it was a case of using the same needle many times.

After nearly two years we were moved to another camp on the outskirts of Shanghai where we stayed for the remainder of the war. There were no flush toilets in this camp and holes in the ground had to be used. Once again there were very few showers and water was always rationed. We all lived in dormitories and the food was worse than ever, both in quality and quantity.

Throughout those years of captivity there were many rumours and one never knew what was true and this of course added to the tension for the adults. Just a couple of months before the war ended it was rumoured that gas chambers were being built and that we were all going to be killed once Japan had won the war. There was also the constant fear of not knowing what the Japanese guards would do when they got drunk.

I remember quite clearly the day I discovered the war had ended. I could understand a little of the Chinese language and had been speaking to some of the Chinese people outside the camp gates. They asked why we were still in camp as the war had ended. I ran to tell my Mother who got very angry with me as the adults had been warned that anybody caught spreading rumours would be severely punished. She was afraid that the Japanese authorities would think that it was my father who had told me to say the war had ended. That same day the Japanese guards became very agitated and started running about getting rid of things and eventually they left the camp. We all went up on to the roof of our camp building and saw two war ships coming up the river to Shanghai. One was American and the other British and I remember thinking that we were now going to be safe.

From 15th August to approximately November 1945 we remained in the camp waiting to be repatriated to the UK by sea. During this period a lot of people became ill. We were getting food from the Americans who had liberated us which was too rich after two and a half years on what was practically a starvation diet. I myself got an abscess under my arm and was very ill because the poison had started to spread all through my body.

At different stages of my life I have had memories stirred; things long forgotten, but when reminded, have caused me a great deal of distress. In 1994 my husband and I went on a tour to China. One of the places we visited was Shanghai. The guide very kindly took us to the road where the first camp had been. The buildings had since been demolished but on that occasion I became very upset as the bad memories came back to me. The memories of those days will stay with me for the rest of my life.

But the good side is that it has made me, I think, a stronger person than I would otherwise have been. When I have had difficult decisions to make or something unpleasant has arisen, I have always said to myself, 'Don't worry. Nothing can be as bad as the camp.' And this has always helped me along life's road.

PART III
The Thai-Burma Railway

Wampo: The Largest Viaduct on the Line

The viaduct at Wampo is still in use. Concrete bases have been added at the foot of the uprights. - G S Gimson

JAPANESE HOLIDAY
Padre J N Duckworth

Padre J N Duckworth's talk, 'Japanese Holiday', was broadcast from Singapore on 12th September 1945.

The Japanese told us we were going to a health resort. We were delighted. They told us to take pianos and gramophone records; they would supply the gramophones. We were overjoyed and we took them. Dwindling rations and a heavy toll of sickness were beginning to play on our fraying nerves and emaciated bodies. It all seemed like a bolt from the tedium of life behind barbed wire in Changi. They said, 'Send the sick. It will do them good.' And we believed them, so we took them all.

The first stage of the journey to this new-found Japanese Paradise was not so promising. Yes, they took our kit and they took our bodies - the whole lot, in metal goods wagons - thirty-five men per truck, through Malaya's beating, relentless sun for free. For food, we had a small amount of rice and some 'hogwash' called stew. We sat and sweated, fainted and hoped. Then at Bampong station in Thailand they said, 'All men go. *Marchee, Marchee!*' We said, 'What! We're coming for a holiday.' They just laughed in that spiteful, derisive scornful laugh which only a prisoner of war in Japanese hands can understand. We knew that here was another piece of Japanese *Bushido* - deceit.

Our party marched, or rather dragged themselves, for seventeen weary nights, 220 miles through the jungles of Thailand. Sodden to the skin, up to our middles in mud, broken in body, helping each other as best we could, we were still undefeated in spirit. Night after night each man nursed in his heart the bitter anger of resentment. As we lay down in the open camps - clearings in the jungle, nothing more - we kept dreaming of home and better things. As we ate boiled rice and drank onion water we thought of eggs and bacon.

We arrived, 1,680 strong at No 2 Camp, Sangria, Thailand, which will stand out as the horror hell of Prison Camps. From this 1,680 less than 250 survived to tell its tale. Our accommodation consisted of bamboo huts without roofs. The monsoon had begun and the rain beat down. We were set to work - slave work - piling earth and stones in little skips onto a railway embankment. It began at 5 o'clock in the morning and finished at 9 o'clock at night and even later. Exhausted, starved and benumbed in spirit we toiled, because if we did not, we, and our sick, would starve. As it was, the sick had half rations because the Japanese said, 'No work, no food.'

Then came cholera. This turns a full-grown man into an emaciated skeleton overnight. Twenty, thirty, forty and fifty deaths were the order of the day. The medical kit we had brought could not come with us. We were told it would come on. It never did. We improvised bamboo holders for saline transfusions, and used boiled river water and common salt to put into the veins of the victims. Cholera raged. The Japanese laughed and asked, 'How many dead men?' We still had to work, and work harder. Presently came dysentery and beriberi, that dreaded disease bred of malnutrition and starvation. Tropical ulcers, diphtheria, mumps and smallpox all added to the misery and squalor of the camp on the hillside where water flowed unceasingly through the huts. A rising feeling of resentment against the Japanese, the weather, and general living conditions, coupled with the knowledge that the officers could do nothing or little about it, made life in the camp full of dread that each day would bring something worse. The lowest daily death rate came down to seventeen only as late as September 1943 when the weather improved and things began to get a little better. Yet we had to work; there was no way out of it. Escape through the jungle, as many gallant parties attempted, would only end in starvation and disease, and if the party survived and was eventually captured, the torture which followed was worse than death itself.

We were dragged out by the hair to go to work, beaten with bamboo poles and mocked at. We toiled, half-naked in the cold, unfriendly rain of Upper Thailand. We had no time to wash and if we did it meant cholera. By day we never saw our bed space (on long platforms of those bleak hundred metre huts). Our comrades died, we could not honour them even at the graveside because we were still working.

The spirit of the jungle hovered over this 'Valley of the Shadow of Death' and my boys used to ask me constantly, 'How long now Padre? What's the news?' We had the news. Captain James Mudie who now broadcasts from here, by an amazing piece of skill and resource, got it and gave it to us. And we lay and starved, suffered, hoped and prayed. Never in my life have I seen such tragic gallantry as was shown by those men who lay on the bamboo slats and I speak now as a priest who ministered the last rites to all of them.

Yet they died happy. Yes, happy to be released from pain. Happy because our cause would not be suffered to fail the nations of this earth. No medical officers or orderlies had to contend with such fantastic, sickening, soul-destroying conditions of human ailment. No body of men could have done better. We sank low in spirit, in sickness and in human conduct, but over that dark valley there rose the sun of hope which warmed shrunken frames and wearied souls.

One cheering result comes from this dismal epoch in our lives: the coming close together in friendship and mutual understanding of the men of the UK and the men of Australia. A new understanding has been born and will endure amongst those who think over things which are of good report. Those of us who came out of that hell thank God for deliverance and for the memory of just men made perfect, men whose example as martyrs at the hands of the Japanese blaze yet another trail in the annals of human perseverance.

SNAPSHOT

One day while a group of RAF prisoners were toiling to build an airfield, a Japanese light bomber landed for fuel, taxiing close to where the men were working. While awaiting fuel, the pilot stood nearby smoking a cigarette. The plane resembled a RAF Blenheim light bomber. One of the prisoners, a Blenheim pilot, casually suggested that the four of them jump the Japanese pilot, hijack the plane and make a dash for Australia. Just as they were about to carry out the plan, the Japanese pilot turned toward them, patted his holstered service revolver and in perfect English with a pronounced American accent said, 'Forget it.' He climbed back into his plane and taxied away. They could only surmise that he was a *nisei*, a Japanese born in the United States, who had returned to fight for the emperor.

28 Dec 1942

Train Journey, Singapore to Thailand

The great majority of about 50,000 POWs sent to build the notorious Siam-Burma Railway travelled in this way, crowded thirty-one to a steel box-car, packed close together, with no room for any to lie down, and no way of getting kit out of the way. The journey took five days and nights, the steel cars burning hot in the tropical sun by day and ice-cold and wet with condensation by night. Food was minimal and appeared on only a few occasions. Most POWs were troubled by one or other of many causes of diarrhoea, with obvious consequences at the rare stops or between them. Their immediate destination was a partly-flooded and hopelessly insanitary camp at the town of BAN PONG (well-named!). - G S Gimson

THE THAI-BURMA RAILWAY
Fred Seiker, Merchant Navy

To supply their army in Burma and avoid the long sea passage around the Malayan peninsula which had been made hazardous by the action of American submarines, the Japanese decided to build a connecting rail link between Bangkok in Thailand and Moulmein in Burma. The route, 260 miles long, was through mountainous jungle which was among the most impenetrable and unhealthy in the world. The route was begun in July 1942 and completed in October 1943. Sixty-one thousand British, Australian and Dutch troops and 270,000 native labourers from Burma, Malaya, Thailand and the Netherlands East Indies worked on the railway. In all 12,000 British and 90,000 of other nationalities died. Despite the extraordinary engineering feat, the railway failed to carry the tonnage expected and was abandoned in early 1945 following Allied bombing. Below is the first part of a talk given by Fred Seiker, Merchant Navy, in 1997; the second part, 'Then Hiroshima Happened!' appears towards the final part of this book.

When asked to talk about 'Life on the Railway' I felt somewhat uneasy about this title because it suggests that there was indeed life during the construction of the Thai-Burma Railway. By that I mean life as I had known it prior to becoming a prisoner of war of the lmperial Japanese Army. Also, to describe the Railway to the uninitiated and expect them to even begin to understand must rank among the 'impossibles' of our time. The mind cannot accept what it hears. I am enlightening you with this to emphasise my understanding of the public's reaction to the stories told about the Thai-Burma Railway, built during the Second World War by Allied prisoners of war. I have, therefore, decided to base this talk on a few personal experiences and witnessed events, avoiding the horrors of the well-documented tortures carried out by the IJA and their military police, the *Kempi Tai*. Those atrocities were executed by the Japanese with relish and often with immense amusement. I would also stress that any opinions about the IJA that might surface during this talk are entirely my own and, by their nature, highly prejudiced.

I became a POW in Bandung, Java, soon after the Japanese occupied the island. I walked into the POW camp, complete with two suitcases filled with all manner of food. The cases were immediately ripped from my grasp, my objections to this act of piracy were rejected by Japanese fists slamming into my face and a rifle butt sending me crashing to the ground. A Japanese officer explained to me in English that I was now a POW of the IJA and, as such, had no rights whatsoever. They then proceeded to remove my personal belongings: watch, photographs and money. The humiliation was complete. In minutes I ceased to be a person. I believe to this day that they considered a worm in the earth of greater value than a POW.

I was shown my temporary quarters consisting of the veranda of an abandoned bungalow which I shared with two other POWs. The veranda was open to the elements and somewhat draughty and wet at times. We soon organised ourselves in some sort of routine and waited for things to develop.

One late afternoon the entire camp was ordered on parade. We were confronted with the spectacle of three sailors, each tied to a wooden pole. A Japanese officer explained that these three chaps had escaped from the camp, but were soon caught and were now waiting to be executed. A rumble rippled through the assembled POWs. It was a tense moment, but the cocked machine guns, trained on us, soon calmed things down. The sailors were executed by bayonet thrusts in the throat, the stomach and lower abdomen. Their death was designed to be painful and slow. A warning to future escapees! It also became clear to us what kind of thugs we were dealing with.

One evening it was announced that we would be taken to another place where we would be put to work on building a railroad. Those who followed orders would be well treated: others would receive harsh but just treatment. Convoys of lorries took us to Tandjong Priok, the harbour of what was then Batavia, now Djakarta. We were herded onto a shabby old rust bucket and driven into the holds of the ... *Maru*. When describing such a scene, even an imaginative mind must fail to grasp the horror of it all. We were stacked - and I mean stacked - onto elevated platforms within the holds of the vessel. The horizontal space per man was just enough to turn over without landing on your neighbour. In some cases bodies had to turn over in unison to avoid landing on the mate next to them. Vertical space was not quite enough to sit up. A dim light at the end of each row of bodies was the only glimmer that could be seen. Each hold had one single opening at the top for ventilation. At each of the openings stood a Jap guard in total command of who was allowed on deck for natural functions. If he decided not to allow you on deck, you were confronted with a huge bayonet, and a hasty retreat back into hell followed. The natural function then took place in the hold: the first dysentery cases began to appear.

The trip to Singapore took several days. Our misery and humiliation at that time was total. On arrival in Singapore we were transported to Changi Jail. Time at Changi was not too bad. The Japs left us alone and we ran our own affairs as best as we could. Food was lousy of course, but little extras could be obtained through various obscure channels. We were obviously waiting for further orders from the Japs. Time was on our hands, and tempers often flared.

Then the time came when we were transported to Thailand. We found ourselves packed into steel railway trucks. I shall not describe our journey which took several days. Various books on the subject have been published describing this hell on wheels in some detail. We eventually arrived at a place called Kanchanaburi where we were housed in a long bamboo hut. The floor consisted of mud, the sleeping platforms were constructed from bamboo slats, the allocated space per man was about two feet, and the roof in many places was open to the sky. This was to be our home for some time to come. It soon became evident that the question of camp and personal hygiene was crucial to one's survival.

I wish to mention something here which is usually avoided in the many books written about this episode. The large base camps in the south of Thailand held thousands of men from various countries, each country with its own distinctive way of life. The British had their community spirit, the Australians their egalitarian attitude, the Dutch their individualism. (The Americans were not in evidence at that time.) It should, therefore, not be too surprising to hear that in the days of early captivity ugly scenes took place among the POWs. Fist fights were the order of the day until we realised that the Japs took great delight in our squabbles. The camp atmosphere then changed for the better and we came to realise that we depended upon each other.

Our group was soon put to work on the foundations for the Kwai Bridge at Tamarkan. We were detailed to work on driving wooden piles into the riverbed for the foundations of the concrete bridge supports. I would like to explain how this highly complex and technical feat was executed. Several triangular wooden pole structures were erected which carried a pulley at the top. A stout rope was fed over the pulley. One end of the rope carried a heavy steel ram: the other one was splayed into several leaders which were held by POWs standing in the river bed. Straight tree trunks were obtained from the surrounding forest, transported to the bridge site by elephants or floated from up-country downstream. A Jap decided which ones were to be used for piling. The piles were hauled into position beneath the ram, and we began pile-driving on the command of a Jap standing on the riverbank shouting through a megaphone the required rhythm at which he decided that piling should take place.

TAMAKAN
5·4·'43

Tamarkan Bridge

*Tamarkan Bridge was the **real** bridge which was not over the River Kwai (Kwae-noi) but over the River Me-Khlong, some two miles from its junction with the Kwai. It was built almost entirely without mechanical aids, to the exact dimensions of a bridge in Java. The steelwork, shipped to Thailand as the Japanese were very short of steel, was erected on the concrete piers shown here. The bridge carried only a small fraction of its intended traffic and was ultimately put out of action by the RAF in June 1945. - G S Gimson*

You pulled in unison, you let go in unison. *'Ichi, ni, san, si, ichi, ni, san, si,'* on and on and on. Hour after hour after hour. Day in, day out. From dawn to dusk, unrelenting. On returning to camp at night it was often difficult to raise the spoon to eat the slop issued to us. Your arms protested in pain, often preventing you from snatching some precious sleep. And yet, come dawn you repeated the misery of the previous day. I often wondered about the miracle of the human body and mind. Believe me, it is quite awesome.

I was fortunate in that I was engaged in the piling operation for only a short while when our group was taken up-country to begin work on the rail embankment. This meant we were to occupy smaller camps run by Japanese non-commissioned officers. These thugs were usually power-drunk, sadistic, evil individuals.

Building embankments consisted of carrying earth from alongside the track to the top of the ever-growing embankment. You carried a basket from the digging area to the top of the embankment, emptied it, and down again to be filled for your next trip up the hill. Or you carried a stretcher - two bamboo poles pushed through an empty rice sack - one chap at each end, and off you went. Simple really. But in reality this job was far from easy. The slopes of the embankments consisted of loose earth. Clambering to the top was a case of sliding and slithering with a weight of earth in attendance. This proved to be very tiring and painful on thigh muscles, often resulting in crippling cramp. You just had to stop, you could not move. Whenever this occurred the Japs were on you with their heavy sticks and beat the living daylight out of you. Somehow you got going again, if only to escape the blows.

The soil alongside the track varied considerably, affecting the volume of earth an individual could move during a day. At the start of each day a Jap would decide the total volume of earth to be dug out that day. By the nature of things, some finished earlier than others. The volume the following day was fixed by the fastest time obtained the previous day, thereby increasing the total workload of the entire team. It was truly a 'no win situation'. If a team was running late, everyone worked on until the volume for that day was achieved. This meant that the Japs also had to stay behind. They relieved their anger and frustration by random beatings of POWs, sometimes resulting in serious injuries.

I have often been asked, 'Can you describe a typical day?' A typical day! A typical day would begin the previous evening at the roll call on return from the work site. The numbers counted then were expected to turn up for work the following morning, with no account taken of those who had become ill, some badly.

It was a never-changing scenario. The orderly who presented the Japs with his sick list was always, and I mean always, beaten up in a show of Jap rage. The poor, sick individuals were then dragged from the so-called hospital and forced to turn out for work on the railway. Sometimes they returned to the camp that night, carried on a sack stretcher, dead! These were, by no means, isolated incidents: they occurred on a daily basis all along the rail track.

I want to express an opinion which is close to my heart. As we know, numerous individuals have been praised and honoured for their humanitarian work in the base camps, often enduring horrendous treatment by the Japs for ignoring their stupid orders. These individuals deserve our admiration and deepest respect. The orderly in the jungle camp carried out his work with steadfast dedication. Day in, day out, he protected his charges with unstinting valour, often moving with great pain in his body from the beatings he received. He knew for certain that every time he tried to protect his mates he would receive a merciless beating. He never flinched, although he did not know whether he would be able to walk away from the next beating. That to me is heroism of the highest order. Where are these men now? I do not recall seeing their names in the lists of honours.

SNAPSHOT
Building a railway was thirsty work and there was often a four-gallon petrol can of well-stewed tea around the cookhouse. Our drinking utensils were usually old tin cans with a handle soldered on and Jap sentries were not in much better shape. One day, a Jap handed his can into the cookhouse and pointed halfway up. '*Hambon*' (half), he said. He got it back cut down to half size - he'd handed it to the camp tinsmith.

I have been intrigued by ex-POWs who readily remember the names of Japs and the camps they occupied. Perhaps this is because I was never long in a particular camp to become familiar with their names, although I must say that the names of the guards never did have much significance for me. However, there is always the exception and one is 'Horseface'. The reason for this nickname becomes obvious when you look at the sketch of his face replicated in my modest book of drawings *Lest We Forget*. He was a Korean guard of the worst type. Many Koreans were sent by the Japs to the smaller camps in which I so often found myself. This thug is the only one I would love to meet on my own ground, even at the amiable age of eighty-two. He was the original pervert and sadist. His main enjoyment was that of loitering at the tail end of a column of POWs returning from a day's slavery on the railway and prodding any straggler with his bayonet, the point of which he had honed to a razor sharp edge. It never caused serious damage, but it always drew a trickle of blood. On spotting the blood he would grunt with pleasure, face distorted in ecstasy. He would then select his next victim. Oh yes, I'd love to win him in a raffle.

I would like to demonstrate to you the crazy philosophy of the Japs and Koreans by referring to what I call the 'kitchen incident'. In one camp in the north of Thailand it occurred that it was my turn to raid the Jap cookhouse in the hope of finding something to eat. It was known to us that the Japs had confiscated a consignment of Red Cross parcels in keeping with their usual procedure. I was able to nick a tin of fruit. On my way back to my eagerly waiting mates, I was suddenly confronted with a glistening bayonet, followed by a kick in the groin. I was terrified. I was marched to the guardhouse with the bayonet in close attendance.

The ritual beating began. Several of the guards pounced on me all at the same time. When eventually the sergeant in charge of the camp appeared, he ordered them to stop. I could not have been a pretty sight; I certainly did not feel like one. He drew his sword and pointed it at my neck, grinning. He addressed me in broken English from which I understood that stealing from the IJA was a serious crime and would be punished by chopping my head off. At some point, I managed to explain to him that I could not possibly be a thief by having taken something that was mine in the first place. He did not appreciate the logic of my defence, and he ordered that I be taken to the punishment tree some ten yards in front of the guardhouse. I had watched many a comrade undergo the sergeant's favourite punishment and realised that it was now my turn. I was propped against the tree, my arms pulled back and tied at the wrists behind the tree trunk. My feet were tied together with barbed wire and secured to the tree trunk. After a few more punches in the face, they left me alone. The pain that lashes your body after a while I must leave to your imagination. When morning broke they put a bucket filled to the brim with water in front of me and left me to it. A sophisticated torture if ever there was one. Parade was called. It was explained that this was the punishment for stealing from the IJA, and that I would be executed later on.

I do not remember much after that. As you are aware by now, the execution did not take place. The terror of it was that you never knew whether it was an idle threat or an official statement. I came to in the 'hospital' with an orderly trying to pour water into my mouth. I have never found out why I was caught, though there was a suspicion. These things did happen now and then. A short while after that I was back on the railway.

Cholera! Once you have lived through a cholera epidemic in a Japanese POW camp you do not have to be afraid of ever finding yourself in hell. There would be no purpose: you have been there and worse. It broke out as suddenly as it vanished. Overnight the huts were filled with the dead and the dying. The Japs were terrified of this disease and hastily retreated a safe distance up the road after barricading the entrance to the camp with X-shaped barricades and rolls of barbed wire. We were instructed to incinerate our dead, not to bury them. Cholera strikes swiftly without warning. It is terminal in the absence of medication. Our medic's kit did not even contain an Aspirin tablet. Combined with the emaciated state we were in, the onslaught was terrifying. You could be OK in the morning and dead in the evening. Once dehydration set in, your place on the pyre was assured.

I was one of a team attending the funeral pyre for a while, and depositing the bodies of my friends into the flames. This was a round-the-clock operation, twenty-four hours a day. It was particularly macabre and frightening at first. Bodies would suddenly sit up, or an arm or leg would extend jerkily. But even this horror soon became a routine job. The cholera outbreak lasted for several horrendous days. It took away many of my friends; I do not recall the total death toll. I learned after the war that some native labour camps were entirely wiped out because of cholera.

On the subject of the acceptance of death, I would like to recall a typical incident. Once, after a day's work on the embankment, a mate next to me lay down for the night's rest, turned to me and said, 'I feel lousy and very tired.' The following morning I shook him to make sure he was awake. He was not, however. He was dead. Died during the night. Quietly. The orderlies came and took him away. Another identity tag into the rusty metal tin! At some time during the day, someone would say, 'Where is old Tony?' The reply would be, 'He's had it, packed up last night.' Someone would mutter 'Lucky bastard, he's out of it.' There never was intended disrespect. Death had become an accepted part of our existence on the Railway of Death.

The railway was completed on 17th October 1943 at Konkuita in Thailand, not far from the Three Pagodas Pass. I shall not enter into the statistics or technical data or the final death toll of the various countries involved (these have been extensively quoted in numerous publications) except to state that the railway was 415 kilometres long and built from scratch in just sixteen months. A previous assessment, carried out by British Engineers, was five years! The total labour force consisted of about 61,000 Allied POWs and 270,000 Asian labourers. The combined death toll was around 100,000, of which 18,000 were Allied POWs. Consider for just a moment how these human beings died, where they died, and, above all, why they died.

When the Railway was completed, teams of maintenance workers were formed by the Japs. These teams moved up and down the track repairing and maintaining bridges, tracks and embankments. I was one of a group sent to northern Thailand and into Burma to dig caves into the hillsides. These caves were used by the Japs for ammunition storage. The caves, connected to the railway by heavily camouflaged roads, were not visible from the air. We often considered the danger we represented to the Japs because of our knowledge of the whereabouts of these caves. It seemed not to bother them. At some point we were ordered to dig tank traps in close proximity to our camp. Tank traps in the middle of virgin jungle? These tank traps were of considerable length and width. Then someone offered the thought that these tank traps looked remarkably like mass graves. I have no personal knowledge of this, but it would appear that later evidence proved the Japanese intent to massacre our group in the tank traps and bulldoze earth over the remains. We would have disappeared forever.

(Continued in Part VI: 'And Then Hiroshima Happened')

SNAPSHOT
From December 1944 when we had completed the railway, our own planes, flying from northern Burma, began to appear and to bomb the bridges. A very large bomber flew low over a working party and the Jap sentry was impressed. '*Taksan* - very big. How many men?' 'Twenty men,' volunteered a POW helpfully. 'Twenty men-*ka*? How twenty?' The POW replied, 'Two men driver, two men *looksee*, two men chop wood, two men carry water, two men *sweejiba* (cookhouse).' The Jap scratched with his stick in the dust. 'Only ten men,' he said puzzled. '*Ahsoga*,' was the reply. 'Other ten *yasume* (rest) *soon changey-changey*.' Later some Guards became more familiar with our planes. One Korean was heard to explain, 'Him no bang-bang. Him come see, go back speak plane.'

Preparing the Trace in Bamboo Jungle

The men worked more or less naked, with poor quality tools. They were shouted at and beaten with bamboo rods or rifle-butts by the Japanese or Korean sentries. The jungle bamboo was sharp-edged and spiny: cuts almost invariably became septic. Little mercy was shown to exhausted or sick men, and daily quotas had to be met. - Watercolour by Jack B Chalker

AFTERTHOUGHTS

Dr George A Graham, formerly of Kilconquhar

We moved to the railway station and on the way there were the heads of Chinese stuck on the tops of long poles. Presumably their owners had been caught in some misdemeanour. We were not very impressed with our transport: cattle trucks to accommodate six cattle. We were allotted twenty-four to a truck along with all our worldly possessions. Discomfort would be quite an understatement: we all sat on our kit for which there was no room otherwise, and only some at a time could lie down.

The journey, which should have taken three days, took four weeks, for on the border of Thailand, the incessant rain had washed away an embankment which we were ordered to repair. At our halt at Bampong, to the west of Bangkok, we managed to buy a water buffalo which would normally be used for drawing a plough to prepare a field for planting rice. The beast was soon killed and roasted, providing many steaks. The smell of these grilling in front of hot fires was wonderful but we were quite disillusioned to find that they were so tough that they were inedible.

Bampong was a transit camp, a place of appalling hygiene not helped by almost continuous rain. Everywhere was a waterlogged bog; latrines were flooded to the brim and excrement was floating around. We were wet, unwashed, sweating and smelly. Food was the usual boiled rice and water 'stew' with occasional bits of meat or vegetable floating around.

Then a fleet of lorries arrived and we were herded like sheep and taken to Chungkai, a large base camp near the junction of two rivers. Here we were told we were to build a railway from Bangkok to Moulmein to provide the Japanese with a line of supply to Burma in order to avoid Allied submarines round the Malay peninsula.

The route of the railway had obviously been surveyed beforehand and roughly followed the river. The track was carved through jungle over very uneven ground, never flat for long and getting much worse as we went further up river. Under the conditions we lived in it was difficult to appreciate the beauty of the scene all around us. Unlimited jungle lay beyond the river on each side. Soon, away from the river, the jungle became denser but very swampy with beautiful trees and even more beautiful groves of bamboo, sometimes up to a height of thirty feet, with close stems spreading out above, and gracefully leaning over to touch the next group of bamboos. Bamboo canes could be up to nine inches in diameter and were used to fashion many articles such as drinking cups and furniture. Across the river were chattering monkeys and I can recall the beautiful flocks of butterflies of many different colours, the kingfisher birds, and the incessant noise of insects always greater at night. The trees were tall and stately and many were of great height as if competing to get up to the light.

The railway ran in a north-westerly direction towards Three Pagoda Pass and Burma. Beyond the pass another river began to flow in the opposite direction and another group of POWs made the railway to the Pass, meeting up in due course. I guess at least 40,000 to 50,000 British, Australian and Dutch troops were employed, in addition to several thousand native coolies later brought up from Malaya. These latter had a very high death rate because of their lack of communal spirit and self-help disciplines.

The Japanese engineers were very skilled, and contrary to the film, no help was ever sought from any POW source. The railway was made with a minimum of sophisticated tools. Hardwood trees abounded in the jungle and were cut down and used in construction of bridges and for many other things. I think the only tools used were axes, picks, shovels, saws, *chunkels* (a kind of matchet), crow bars, nails, screws and wire. I saw elephants used for pulling timber for bridges. I saw one piling up timber of equal lengths, standing back occasionally and going forward to adjust the log so that it was flush with those underneath. On another occasion two elephants were pulling a large tree, one on each side with a rope attached to the log. One elephant was obviously lazy and not doing his share of the work. The other put up with this for a while, then picked up a large stick and threw it at the idler.

When building the embankment a squad of troops went in advance, clearing a path through the jungle which had been surveyed by the engineers. These were mainly Northumberland Fusiliers, many of whom were miners from the Durham area. They knew how to appear to be working hard when any supervision was around. Building the embankment was the work of small groups armed with picks, shovels, matchets and carrying baskets for the soil. Each small gang was overseen by a Jap armed with a rifle. There was a lot of sabotage: slipshod work and bamboo roots put in surreptitiously in the embankment with the hope that they would eventually grow out and be a nuisance. There was a continual row about the speed of working and the supervising engineers were a vicious lot. They in turn would take it out on the Japanese guard if they were not satisfied. Accelerated rates of working were called for regularly: we called them '*speedos*'.

There were two large groups of POWs making the railway. Each group was split into smaller parties. Our group was responsible for the first twenty miles or so and when this was completed we leap-frogged the other group and did the section beyond. The railway itself, over very difficult terrain, was a succession of embankments, bridges and culverts. The ground was very uneven with little valleys running into the main river.

Wan Lun (or One Lung to us) was my first stop and here I met my first medical problem. Ours was a camp of 1,200 men with three doctors of whom I was the senior. In one hut, out of about five, we noticed a few sore throats; then it became obvious we had diphtheria. Over the next three or four weeks we had a number of cases. The Japs ordered them down river to Chungkai where they infected others and started an epidemic. The death rate was about fifty per cent.

The weather in Thailand consists of a rainy season and a less rainy season when there was a good deal of sunshine. In the rainy season it could rain steadily all day and all night for a week on end and it could be quite cold at night. This made for slippery mud everywhere and it was unintentionally messy around the latrines, the mess being increased by the water level in the latrines rising. Most of the time the weather suited us as there was little need for clothing. The temperature was around ninety to ninety-two degrees during the day with high humidity, and in the rainy season, cold at nights.

Most troops wore what we called a 'G' string - a string around the waist holding in place a bit of cloth attached to the string over the buttocks and passing between the legs around the crutch, then doubled over the string at the front. A hat or head covering of some kind was essential as we were much in the sun. Our skin got used to sun and only the blonds and the redheads suffered, especially on the shoulder where the burn gave a chronic crusted rash. Footwear was a problem and most of us used 'flip-flops', moulded wooden soles with a strap across, usually from an old tyre.

Disease was chronic and nobody escaped some problem. Malaria was the commonest and was rife and relatively uncontrolled. There were small, infrequent and inconsistent issues of quinine given out by the Japs; and yet Java, probably the world's greatest source of quinine was in Japanese hands. I had malaria about seven times and considered myself lucky: it was most probably benign tertian with rigors at forty-eight hour intervals. Without microscope evidence it was impossible to know definitely the type of malaria. Many people with frequent recurrences had grossly enlarged spleens, and at that stage anaemia was common, sometimes extreme with great loss of weight. The anaemia and debility made those affected prone to other problems, or exaggerated them, but I was never laid up for longer than a part of a day at a time. Dengue fever, an influenza-like pyrexical illness, was common and this I had once.

Amoebic and bacillary dysentery were endemic and there was no means of identifying the cause of blood and mucus in the stools: they were only distinguished by gross clinical features. Either alone or following upon malaria, either of these could well be fatal. I once passed a stool with blood and mucus and feared the worst, but next day all was well and there was no repetition. Diarrhoea was the rule (fortunately I was an exception) and probably connected with our diet of mainly rice and watery stews.

Beriberi, pellagra and other vitamin-deficiency diseases were a way of life. The main symptom of beriberi (vitamin B1 deficiency) was swelling of the feet, ankles and lower leg, possibly going on to congestive heart failure. Dry beriberi produced polyneuritis and muscle weakness, then wasting. Pellagra (deficiency of vitamin niacin or nicotinic acid) produced skin lesions, especially in parts exposed to the sun, progressing to nervous or mental disorder, quite commonly also associated with an exuding dermatitis of the scrotum, and given by us the rather picturesque name of 'rice balls'. On one occasion I can remember I complained to the Japanese sergeant who was reputedly the equivalent of a sergeant in the RAMC, the 'medical' authority controlling the health of some 1,500 of us, about the problem. I was asked, 'How many?' I said, 'Lots', and was thereupon ordered to produce them which I did: about twenty in all. They had to line up for the sergeant to inspect and confirm. The sergeant then said that the Japanese had a simple cure and he got a long stick with a large swab attached to the end. He dipped this into methylated spirit, or some such spirit, and painted each scrotum. You can imagine the exquisite agony, the shouts of protest and the bad language of the victims!

Leg ulcers were very common and any cut or abrasion of the leg easily became septic and then a chronic ulcer ensued. A lot of trouble came from bamboo. There was one type of bamboo which had spike-like thorns, and with no covering for the legs, wounds and scratches easily appeared. These were very difficult to heal and with the body in a debilitated state they soon became septic and an ulcer formed. Some of these got to enormous proportions, often encircling the whole calf, and under normal conditions would qualify for a skin graft. These large ulcers increased a person's debility which coming from several causes, would slowly lead to death in an emaciated state. The death rate from all causes was over 30%.

At the commencement of captivity it was envisaged that body lice would be a problem, but as it turned out, the lack of clothes in a warm climate acted against the spread of lice. Some were found but the problem was not great. Bed bugs on the other hand were a perpetual source of trouble: they were in the corners of mosquito nets, in the seams of clothing, in the bamboo slats of bed platforms and anywhere else they could hide. They had a characteristic nasty smell when crushed; blood which had come from the person bitten was obvious. A regular search was a necessary routine and on every tenth day, an official 'holiday' unless it was cancelled, this was done and where possible articles would be held over a fire which would bring the bugs out. They were then killed more easily. Not in the same category, and not so common but also a painful nuisance, were scorpions which produced a nasty sting and were apt to lurk in boots and other unexpected places, and one had to be careful.

Though we saw a lot of snakes, they were not a problem. I never had to treat a case of snakebite. When we caught snakes we often cooked them. The taste was not unpleasant, rather like rabbit without as much taste, and much improved with garlic and salt, both of which were obtainable.

Depression as a primary condition was not a feature and I cannot remember a case of suicide, although I do know that the occasional case happened elsewhere.

Cholera produced a devastating effect. It is endemic seasonally in Thailand in the rainy season when it is carried in the water of swollen rivers, and we lived always beside the river. Despite warnings, POWs would wash, bathe and clean dishes in the river. It was difficult to know when the epidemic started but there would be a sudden increase in the death rate, together with the typical symptoms of vomiting and profuse diarrhoea. When it became obvious, we solicited Japanese help with diagnosis and treatment but we got none. Segregation of those affected was the best they could advise. So we embarked upon this. We made another camp at some distance from the main camp and huts were erected to accommodate those affected. Being Senior Medical Officer I got the four other doctors to draw lots to see who would stay with the sick and it fell to the lot of a Manchester chap called Braham. Braham was later to disappear, presumably drowned, when the ship carrying him to Japan was sunk.

The cholera epidemic happened while we were at 211 Kilo Camp in 1944. It lasted a couple of months and claimed around 200 lives. It progressed despite all sorts of measures to contain it. 'Treatment' was simply by frequent sips of fluid with salt and sugar added in small amounts. Intramuscular boiled and filtered saline was tried but soon stopped owing to some nasty cases of cellulitis. We did not dare to try intravenous fluids. I can remember a strong, apparently healthy officer whom I saw in good condition at breakfast. He was dead by lunchtime having had four copious watery motions with massive dehydration resulting.

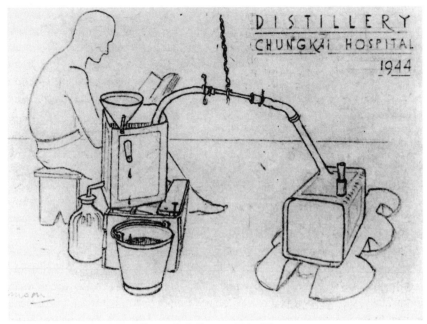

Chungkai Camp: Distillery

The distillery was used to produce sterile water for injection into cholera patients to replace their rapid fluid loss. The normal water supply from the river was both heavily contaminated and full of silt. Distilleries were built from scrap, including rubber tubes from medical officers' stethoscopes. They had to be worked twenty-four hours a day. - G S Gimson

Cholera victims' bodies had to be cremated as they were a great source of possible spread of infection. This was done by rather a macabre group of lads, superintended by Busty Ross and Buch Graham, two lieutenants of the Royal Scots Fusiliers, I think. They were both promoted NCOs of considerable army experience and really genuine chaps, the sort of men I would have chosen to accompany me in any dangerous situation. They made fires of bamboo, not always an easy performance when it could rain without ceasing for several days. The corpse had to be lashed down on the funeral pyre, a method learned from experience because in earlier attempts the body had sat up, and having done so would topple sideways and fall off. This was rather a lurid sight which occurred because the flexor muscles tightened with the heat before the extensors.

The Japanese had great faith in M&B 693 tablets (sulphanilamide) which before the war were having worldwide successful sales. They were at that time, before the advent of penicillin, the most powerful antidote to many disease-producing bacteria. They were a specific remedy against certain bacillary infections such as gonorrhoea from which so many of the Japs suffered. They sought after these as a self-administered remedy. Some enterprising POWs made replicas of these tablets by making moulds and filling them with chalk mixed with an adhesive preparation. They then flogged them to the Japanese sufferers at a good price. I would like to know the outcome.

Another dirty trick was to get a portion of a stool from a dysentery patient and give it to one of the British cooks in the Japanese kitchen to mix surreptitiously with the food they were preparing and dish it up to the Japs. Again I have no record of the result.

It was known that the Japanese Army was based upon the German army. This would explain their fondness for statistics which soon became manifest and it was clear that they made little use of them. It is easier to record than to come to conclusions from the evidence obtained. They asked for a four-monthly register of all who were tattooed. I cannot think what use could be made of that. Another survey was the survey of occupations. As no one would admit to being a coal miner or engineer or even a labourer for fear of being singled out for work of that kind, it must have been surprising to the Japanese that there were so many shop-walkers, beauty specialists, clerks and hairdressers in the British forces.

Although never admitted, our guards were definitely troops considered as unfit for front-line soldiers. They rather despised us because we had given ourselves up without committing *Hara Kiri* as they insisted they would have done. They in turn were despised by the engineers, a battalion of whom were responsible for building the railway, and who were spread out over the whole distance. About five of them supervised the work of our section. We only saw them now and again and their visits usually meant trouble. They were vicious and arrogant and whenever they appeared they usually demanded more labour. Our guards were afraid of them and did their best to put pressure on us.

The 2,200 or so in my camp were looked after by thirty to forty Japanese with two or three NCOs and an officer in charge. One doctor was responsible for the medical administration of the whole group of about 8,000. He was a man called Novasaba who was reported to be a paediatrician in peacetime. He did not give much evidence of knowledge of medicine and was rarely seen. His main purpose seemed to be to get as many of the sick out working as possible. I had the satisfaction subsequently of learning that he had been hanged after trial in Singapore.

In our camp, responsibility for medical affairs was in the hands of a sergeant of their medical corps who answered my protests and pleas with the remark that there was nothing he could do.

As to sanitation, a lot of labouring for this was provided by the small camp staff allowed. The first essential was latrines. These were simply trenches six feet or so long and four to five feet deep with a couple of longitudinal bamboos to prevent the squatter falling in. As we had neither the labour nor the raw material to try fly-proofing, they became a wonderful source of flies and were moving with maggots. I complained, and was ordered by the Jap medical sergeant that everyone in the camp, including the sick, had to produce 200 dead flies for his inspection after the working parties had left. This nonsense went on for two or three weeks. Not surprisingly it had no result.

The river was our lifeline. It was used for washing clothes, cleaning dishes, bathing and washing ourselves. But seasonally it was a poisonous disease producer of cholera. Our food supplies came up by barge belonging to the Thais, most of whom were mildly anti-Japanese. The biggest contractor based at Bampong was called Boon Pong. He did much to produce secret goods and smuggle them into our camps and often paid for things himself. After the war I understand he was recompensed financially and given some kind of honour.

The barge people did a bit of private work on the side producing canteen supplies of eggs, fruit, cigarettes, tobacco and a small quantity of sticky, unrefined sugar. Tobacco was inexpensive as it was grown in Thailand. Bamboo pipes were easily made for smoking. Cigarette paper was improvised from books. The thinnest paper from the pages of bibles was much sought after and could command a good price. Ordinary pages of books could, with some expertise, be split so that two thin pages could be made out of the original page. On one occasion at a higher camp, a herd of wild pigs on the other side of the river, greatly alarmed, possibly by a leopard or tiger, charged into the river and swam across not knowing that our camp was on the other side. They charged through the camp with great squeals. It was surprising how many lethal weapons such as axes, long knives, matchets and even iron bars appeared and how quickly. The pork provided a most welcome addition to our evening meal that memorable day.

As to food, I have no record of the exact amount of food ingredients in our diet. For breakfast we had soft, mushy pap rice with watery 'Chinese' tea made from green leaves. Lunch was boiled rice and vegetable stew with fresh or dried vegetables, again rather watery and occasionally a little meat or fish floating around in it. The evening meal was a thicker stew with a fried 'rissole' made mainly of rice. Being so watery the diet caused chronic diarrhoea.

Our housing was of a fairly universal pattern. Huts were about twenty yards long with a passage or aisle down the centre, roughly three feet wide. On each side there was a raised platform made of flattened-out bamboo which was lashed down on a bamboo frame about three feet from the ground, allowing a man to stretch out with his worldly goods behind. About three feet per man were allotted. The roof was made of attap, or palm fronds, which were placed horizontally and overlapped, preventing most of the rain getting through. We made these huts ourselves and a day was usually allowed for this when we arrived at a new destination.

Bamboo was readily available and lent itself to the manufacture of all sorts of things: water bottles; containers of all sorts; chairs; pipes for smoking; medical instruments; artificial limbs and housing gutters. Bamboo sheeting was made by splitting the bamboo down one side, removing the centre partitions, then opening out and hammering until flat.

Escape was impossible, so great was the distance to be travelled and so difficult the ground, mostly dense jungle, to be crossed. There were few attempts. In one camp I was in, my Irish RAMC sergeant whom I tried to dissuade, went off in a westerly direction with another man, hoping to get to Burma and from there to the sea back to India. He got only a short distance before being caught, presumably given away for money by Thai peasants. I was told later by a guard that they were summarily shot after capture.

The only camp with a perimeter fence was Tamarkan, at the east end of the Bridge over the River Kwai. When the bridge was bombed by our planes it was amazing how quickly and easily the seven foot high perimeter fence was breached by POWs making for safety in the jungle. Unfortunately a stick of bombs fell on the camp killing forty-two POWs.

I was told some years after the war that I was to have been shanghaied by an escape party when we were right up the river at our last camp. Apparently the quartermaster and two others laid by a store of food at some distance from the camp. With the knowledge that we would be leaving soon to go down river when the railway was complete, it was intended that the four of us would disappear. We would then stay in hiding until Malaya and Thailand were invaded by British troops. Fortunately the three changed their minds at the last minute.

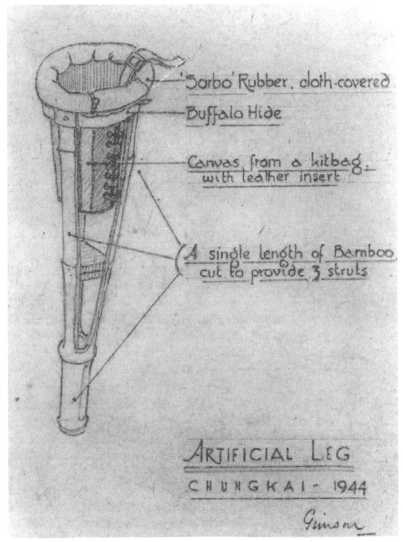

'Sorbo' Rubber. cloth-covered

Buffalo Hide

Canvas from a kitbag.
with leather insert

A single length of Bamboo
cut to provide 3 struts

ARTIFICIAL LEG

CHUNGKAI - 1944

Gimson

Chungkai Camp: Bamboo Artificial Leg, Mark 1, POW Designed

Artificial limbs could be made out of wood and bamboo for those who lost their legs through jungle ulcers. The bamboo, being slightly flexible, made the leg more comfortable. The rubber ring was made from the seat cushions of wrecked vehicles and the leather inserts with lacing were from Dutch officers' leggings. The leg was worn with a harness of webbing straps. Later models, in hardwood, had a hinged knee and ankle. A small number of double-amputees were provided with short 'stumps'. More than 300 amputations were carried out. - G S Gimson

LEE SOON (Alias BOON PONG)
Brian G Brown, Royal Signals

I never met Nai Boon Pong but he was given the credit for providing help to us on the railway. He cashed a postal order for ten shillings for me from the congregation of Bellahouston Parish Church which I had received just before the capitulation. He used to come up the river and would sell all sorts things including, I believe, much needed medicines and certain torch cells for the Webber brothers' wireless built in two water bottles. These certainly gave many of us the will to survive. He was extremely good for the morale and I was told that a decoration was conferred on him after the war. It was well deserved.

I had a letter from R A Westhoff, Estepona, a regular officer in the Navy who was a POW on the railway. Westhoff knew Mr Boon Pong and his wife. According to Westhoff, Mr Boon Pong honoured all *IOUs*. His wife swam our camp moat at night with medical aid around her neck. Westhoff visited them at their home after the Jap surrender and listened to the radio which had been used by Boon Pong to get news for our camp. He was honoured by Britain and his sons were educated at the expense of the Dutch government and the Federation of British Industries.

George Holland from Aberdeen also wrote about Boon Pong. He states that in 1943 he was permitted to set up a canteen selling eggs, sugar and dried fish in Chungkai. This camp, situated up from Kanchanabu, was called Kapoon by the Thais but Chungkai was the name of the family of the market gardeners the Japs had taken the area from to set up the POW Camp. In Chungkai, clothing and effects left behind by those who could no longer be bothered to carry them further up country, as well as the odd pens, watches and trinkets we had still managed to keep from Jap searches, could be bartered for food with the natives. Among the items left behind were violins, a case of light bulbs and even a piano! There were no strings for the violin but Boon Pong was asked by Major Peacock when in Bangkok if he could get us some and a week or two later he brought some in.

According to Holland, 'Boon gave good prices and gave *IOUs* at the rate of a Thai *baht* for one pound. He was able to put us in touch with the civilian camp in Bangkok where money was raised for us by those civilians with outside connections and enabled an underground supply line to be set up. The officers who got paid in *baht* were giving a good amount to the hospital and Boon Pong was trusted with the money to buy eggs and vegetables and slowly he widened his purchases to medicines and cat-gut for the operations as well.

'I was working in the operation room of the hospital and I still have a record of the surgical procedures carried out at Chungkai, Tamarkan and Tamuan camps - over a thousand in all. None was carried out without anaesthetic, mostly spinal, a good amount of which was supplied by the Boon Pong supply line. One item of interest I recall. We had a fair supply of surgical instruments and all was make-do and mend. Our six-man team with Major Pemberton thought out a way to adapt a lumbar drainage tube to use in a colostomy, using a balloon tied to the tube and inflated. We asked for some contraceptives. We had to ask more than once before Bangkok believed us and sent the necessary articles.'

Bangkok Today

Boon Pong died in Bangkok in 1994 at the age of eighty-three. He received the King's Medal for Courage in 1948 and the following year was made an officer of the Order of Orange-Nassau by the Dutch Government.

Tamarkan Bridge: Post-War Photograph

The bridge, repaired, is still in daily use. With forty or fifty miles of additional track going northwards, the railway has proved to be a boon to riverside villagers and to tourists. - G S Gimson

THE BEST OF ENEMIES

Frank Davies, Manchester Club

My squad had been instructed to hack down a thirty-foot tall clump of bamboo on the perilous cliff of rocks and bamboo overlooking the river. We chipped and clawed at it for hours. We dragged it to the river edge. We had to secure it to the riverbed but the Kwai was on the rampage and we hung on grimly as it tried to tear the tree away from us. We were about to let go when I became aware of a small uniformed figure clinging to the tip of the bamboo, twenty feet from the bank. One of our guards had fallen from his perch and only our tree had saved him from being swept to his death. We could have released the bamboo and told the Japanese that their comrade had been the victim of a tragic accident. Instead, as a result of some compelling regard for human life, we found ourselves hauling the bamboo and the terrified guard ashore. He was quaking and seemed convinced that it was I alone who had saved his life.

Later he sought me out in the compound. He spoke of honour and plied me with fruit, fresh eggs, dried fish and cigarettes. Then he bowed and parted with the words, 'You Franko Number One soldier.' My very good friend.' Though I didn't know it at the time, this bizarre declaration of friendship would save my life.

One night I stole out of the compound with a trusted friend and made for a nearby village. There we exchanged watches, pens and items of clothing for food from the hospitable villagers. A modest feast was mustered and we drank cup upon cup of rice wine. After two years of captivity we were so unaccustomed to alcohol that we set off back to the compound hopelessly drunk. Giggling and stumbling we at last reached the hole we had bashed in the compound's bamboo palisade. I was half way through, wriggling on my back, before I realised that someone was pricking my throat with a bayonet. If the camp commandant discovered that we had been fraternising with the locals we were liable to be shot. The pair of us lay there sobered up by fear until the uniformed figure gestured us to get on our feet. I tried to think of something suitably abject to say such as, 'Sorry, I won't do it again': not that that would have done any good. So I shut my eyes, awaited the buffets and insults, and prayed.

After what seemed like an eternity the guard advanced and whispered hoarsely, 'You Franko? Yes?' I opened my eyes. A familiar face was peering into mine but the look was inscrutable. The guard I could tell was pondering. Then I felt a blow across my face and the impact of a boot against my backside. Next moment the guard was gone: we had been spared. I never saw the man again.

That night, you might say, we were the best of enemies.

SNAPSHOT

In October 1942 almost 15,500 left Changi, as did a further 900 from other camps in Singapore. By far the greater number were destined for Bampong and the Burma Railway, but some went to Japan and Formosa whilst a party of 600, under the command of Lieutenant Colonel J A Bassett (35th LAA Regiment, RA) sailed on 18th October for New Guinea. This party arrived at Rabaul on the 5th November, and was then moved to Kokopo. At the end of the month, the 517 men classified as 'fit' were told they were being taken to the Solomon Islands to build an aerodrome. Nothing more was heard of these 517 men. The War Crimes trials refer to evidence given by a Japanese Lieutenant Colonel relating to 517 white prisoners arriving on Ballali Island at the end of 1942, of whom there were no survivors at the end of the war. On Ballali a mass grave containing the remains of 435 bodies was found. Natives on the island told of a massacre of prisoners, the Japanese using bayonets. It would appear that this took place about the time in April 1943 when the Japanese had heard that Allied warships were approaching the island. Of the eighty-three men left behind at Kokopo, only eighteen were to survive to be released in September 1945.

INTELLIGENCE BEHIND BAMBOO

Tom McGowran

We were never completely cut off from the outside world. Soon after the surrender a couple of POWs slipped through the wire at Changi village and came back with enough parts to build a wireless set. When we were moved up to the Burma railway, half a dozen of us took bits of the set with us. As we arrived at Kanchanaburi camp there was a kit inspection. I managed to slip a rheostat out of my kitbag into the mud at my feet and recover it later. Lance Thew, who reassembled the set, was not thrilled at the treatment it had received, but it worked.

A job in one camp was to help get batteries off the Jap lorries at night to operate a set. The Japs twigged what was going on and placed some of us on guard. Needless to say we turned a blind eye, though it nearly cost me my head. As I sat reading by the light of an improvised lamp, supposedly on guard, I heard a noise and looked up in time to see a Jap officer, quite naked, rushing at me with drawn sword. In a rage he screamed that I was neglecting my duty and took a swipe at a bush beside me. I stood with bowed head, braced for the blow. He raged and hacked at the bush until there was nothing left but a stump. Then he calmed down. I reckon if that bush had not been there, it would have been my head.

After the fall of Singapore, the Japs, elated at the richness of their captured city, spared little time to the captured army. Prisoners were herded into a big area on the east side of the island, given bags of rice and told to get on with the business of living. Communication with the outside world ceased; no news filtered through the perimeter fence guarded by Sikh and Jap sentries. As the stunning effects of defeat wore off, this absence of news had a more depressing effect than the absence of food. Men could, and did, eke out their diet with leaves and grass; but the only substitute for authentic news was wild rumour which had a deadly effect on morale.

Faced with the imperative need to steady the troops, one dark night Captain George Haddow from Falkirk and another officer crawled through the fence and managed to buy from a native *kampong* enough wireless parts to build two fairly reliable sets. These were soon working, and early in April 1942 a news service was instituted which continued without interruption until the Jap collapse, despite the efforts of the *Kempi Tai*, the Jap secret police, to break it down. When the move to Siam began in September 1942 for work on the infamous Burma-Siam railway, the sets were dismantled and carried in kit bags to the new camps.

In Siam new problems arose. No longer camped in one big area where inter-camp communication was easy, prisoners were grouped in small parties along the jungle route into Burma. To get the news to camps without wireless, a cipher system was needed. Normally in war, both sides safeguard communications in this way and are aware that the other side is doing the same, and both maintain special departments with the object of breaking the enemy's cipher. In the prisoners' case, the additional problem was to conceal the fact that a cipher was in use at all. A cipher was finally evolved by intelligence officers to carry news in apparently innocent letters between camps.

Resistance work 'inside the fence' fell under four objectives: mapping of Jap defence works and movements of troops; collecting and distributing news by radio and other means; organising for arming and co-ordinating prisoners in the event of an Allied invasion; and enforcing the security measures that made everything else possible.

It is indicative of the scope of the service that when the Jap secret police uncovered one of the wireless sets in use, they also discovered plans relating to the number of Jap troops in Siam and a secret escape road through the jungle, the existence of which was supposed to be known only to a few high-ranking Jap officers. In the resulting 'hate', two officers were beaten to death and several others imprisoned. Throughout that night in the camp the screams of the tortured men put sleep beyond question.

The discovery of this wireless set at Kanchanaburi in central Siam was the result of a breakdown in the security measures. At this time, typed daily bulletins were sent up by the ration train to various camps, concealed in bags of rice. A careless POW 'link' was seen by a Jap taking the news sheet from a bag and the *Kempi Tai's* suspicions were aroused. All camps were searched and the cipher circuit worked overtime, warning officers and men of impending searches and questioning. At the Kanburi camp, the *Kempi Tai* examined as usual all receptacles. One interpreter picked up a biscuit tin, saw that it was apparently full of peanuts and threw it down. The tin broke open and revealed a false bottom in which the set was hidden. The owner was then taken out on to the square and publicly beaten and kicked to death.

Apart from beatings, the Jap inquisition made use of the most picturesque torture methods including the famous medieval 'boot' of Nurnberg when they tried in vain to get Col H H Lilly, 1/5 Forresters, to speak. In the end, by co-ordinating the stories of those questioned, the circuit managed to confine suspicion to the set already discovered. In some cases it was possible to indict Jap sentries who had passed on bits of information.

During this period of upheavals and sudden arrests, the circuit continued its quiet, unobtrusive work.

On another occasion when a set was discovered the operator was more fortunate. A RAF officer was assembling a set at one of the up-country camps and so engrossed was he that he did not realise he was being watched by a Korean sentry. The sentry took the officer before 'Tiger', the Jap NCO in charge of the camp. Always a quick starter, Tiger said, 'You will be shot!' but calmed down when the officer said he had only constructed a few demonstration parts for a series of lectures he was giving. Unfortunately new wireless parts were due to arrive next day by the ration barge which would now certainly be searched. The cipher service got to work and warned down-river camps to intercept the barge and hide their own sets.

As a result of these exposures a new cipher was devised, more flexible than the other, and copies were sent to all camps. Unfortunately about this time the *Kempi Tai* discovered a cipher system in operation among prisoners in Borneo and their attentions increased. It was therefore decided to abolish all written ciphers and substitute a purely 'memory' system. Mark II Star was a simple transposition cipher by which each letter of a clear message was changed into another letter according to a system of numbers based on the date and the decimal for fractions of seven. These decimals have some very peculiar qualities. Each one expressed as a decimal comprises the same six figures in the same sequence. Furthermore, to prevent analysis, a jumbled alphabet was used.

The operators of Star were the first members of a group known as 'The Circuit' which later became a highly organised secret nucleus for resistance work. Each operator went through a cipher course before going out to establish another link in the chain of camps. Operators knew each other only by numbers so that even under torture they were unable to give away secrets. It was a first principle that if an operator were caught it was his responsibility to ensure that suspicion ended with him.

There were some amusing false constructions placed upon the apparently clear letters containing Star information by those not in the circuit. On one occasion a letter to an operator apparently alleging a huge debt to the canteen found its way into the hands of the man's commanding officer who promptly put him on a charge.

Although radio was the most important source of news, friendly Chinese and Thais frequently slipped newspapers in various languages into the camps, together with thousands of dollars. A group of interpreters, known as the 'Brains Trust', was constantly at work translating these papers. An enterprising British batman to some Jap NCOs used to smuggle Jap newspapers nightly from the mess and return them the following morning. At Nakom Patom, the big base hospital camp, newspapers could only be obtained at a Chinese village some way from the camp. Each morning therefore, when the big refuse buckets were taken out of the camp for emptying, a man was concealed under the filth and released beyond the camp. He returned the following morning by the same route bringing newspapers and gossip. This route was also used for the dispatch of letters to friendly Bangkok business houses which sent back money and drugs.

The circuit was also responsible for the organising of escape parties, but the insurmountable obstacles of jungle, hostile natives and lack of food, prevented any of these parties from reaching its goal. The men mostly died in the jungle or were brought back and publicly shot or beheaded after digging their own graves. Towards the end the circuit was taxed to its utmost to keep in touch with the Siamese underground movement which, trained by British and American paratroops who had been in the country secretly for months, planned open revolt against the Japs. The first objective of the Siamese revolt was to be the release of Allied prisoners. Unfortunately the Japs were aware of these plans and had given instructions to Camp Commandants that in the event of trouble, all prisoners were to be executed. The operative date was August 18th 1945, but on the 16th, news leaked through that the Japs had surrendered. The Siamese geared up to fighting pitch were furious with frustration and nerves and took what revenge they could on isolated Jap garrisons. A Korean guard who ventured beyond the perimeter of Pratchai camp came back the following day minus his nose.

Throughout, it had been the aim to contact Allied sources by means of a transmitting set, but although the set was built, sufficient power was never available for its operation. It can be said however, that contact was established by other means and that no event of major importance which took place in enemy occupied country was long a secret from the Allies.

Other radios were in operation throughout the camps in the Far East. During 1942 and early 1943 the POWs in Palembang, Sumatra, were all concentrated in schools and buildings in the town area. Electric power was available and it was not long before radio receiving sets were in operation. This state of affairs was far too dangerous and all sets, except one, were destroyed. Not long after Christmas 1942, a friendly Japanese soldier told a Japanese-speaking British officer that the Japanese Military Police had information about the set still working and strongly advised its immediate destruction. Some of the people concerned were willing to take a chance as they felt that once the set was destroyed it might never be possible to replace it. However, on previous occasions this same friendly Japanese soldier had given information about searches which had proved to be accurate and the Camp Commander ordered that the set should disappear at once. That very night the *Kempi Tai*, Japanese Military Police, descended on the Camp and went straight to the place where the set had been concealed only a few hours previously - up among the rafters of the building. How they got the information nobody knows. Only four men knew where the set was concealed, and they were the operators. It is probable that the Japs found the set by means of some sort of listen-in device.

On the formation of a new camp in the jungle where no electric power was available, and batteries could not be obtained, the news service failed completely apart from wild rumour brought in by troops who had been working along with Indonesians. Six really good men were picked out, one of whom was a highly qualified engineer employed by the Australian Broadcasting Corporation. The party was taken in a truck to the HQ of one of the Jap Army Units and there shown a heap of radio sets which they were ordered to repair. The charade began and they explained to the Japs that they did not know much about that sort of work but the whip was cracked and they were ordered to get on with the work. They removed the 'innards' from one of the sets and in a short time the room was strewn with wire and all the other component parts of a radio receiver. What the Japanese did not know was that the set, in spite of its scattered look, was actually receiving within a very few minutes and the Australian, a sergeant, was making mental notes of all the important items. After about three days the set was re-assembled and the Japanese were delighted to find it in working order and rewarded the men with extra food and cigarettes.

This party continued on the same lines for months and brought back the news faithfully every night. It was not until a War Crimes Trial in Singapore in 1946 that the Japanese knew that the camp was getting real news apart from that issued in the English editions of the Singapore Times which were sometimes supplied to the camp as propaganda.

The worst time was when a few in the camp knew that Japan had capitulated but the news had to be kept from everybody except the few in the inner ring. The Japanese made no sign and the working parties continued. The guards beat up the prisoners as usual. There was just no let-up. Under the circumstances it was quite impossible to risk letting the cat out of the bag as some foolhardy types might have been stupid and lost their own lives as well as those of others. After several days of mental torture the Japs announced that the war was over. It transpired that the reason for the delay was that they were making up their minds whether to fight on. This would have meant the murder of all prisoners.

Chungkai Camp: In Hospital with all Belongings

The man in this drawing has septic ulcers on both shins and is also suffering from beriberi (malnutrition) which caused the bloated appearance of his body. One ulcer was covered with a frequently boiled length of bandage, carefully preserved. In the absence of any other cloth the other is covered with a piece of banana-leaf to keep out flies and dust. His bedding consisted of an army rain-cape and a straw rice-sack; a sweat-rotted shirt and shorts served as a pillow. For clothing he had a cotton G-string ('Jap-happy') and probably a tattered hat, army boots without laces, and for utensils, a half mess-tin, spoon, mug and water-bottle. - G S Gimson

SMILES
Fred Seiker, Merchant Navy

It was the year 1944. Somewhere near the Three Pagoda Pass on the Thai-Burma Border. They had force-marched us from sunrise to sunset for two days. 'Us' being prisoners of war. 'They' being two Japanese soldiers. The group consisted of Dutch and British POWs. We were pronounced 'fit' by a Japanese medical person with the rank of Private, who assured us that we were going for 'short walk, good camp'. Experience told us that this meant 'long walk, no camp'. Ahead of the column strode the Japanese sergeant, our pathfinder and pacesetter. At the rear, a disgruntled Japanese private slouched along, prodding stragglers with a bayonet ridiculously large for the size of the soldier.

The jungle was oppressively hot, humid and dense. We carried our rations, cooking utensils (discarded oil cans) and tools on three makeshift carriers. The carriers were made up from old rice sacks and bamboo poles: a kind of stretcher. Each stretcher was carried by a team of four men. Those with ulcerated legs were not required to be pack mules. This was not a Japanese gesture. It was our decision, after lengthy arguments and several face-slapping sessions from the sergeant. One team was already carrying a man who had collapsed with dysentery. The two remaining teams now had to carry the additional load of the stretcher occupied by the sick man. The sergeant would not allow us to make up a fourth stretcher because he had already given us a concession with regard to the men with ulcerated legs!

We had not drunk a sip of water all day. Our bodies were dried out, our throats were hoarse, our tongues felt like leather strips in our mouths. We were giddy from exhaustion and most of us suffered stomach cramp. The familiar gibbon calls could no longer be heard. It meant there was no fresh water for miles around. We made camp at dusk in a clearing close to a muddy pool alive with insects. Several thrust their faces into the murky water, drinking greedily. Moves to stop them were met with violent objection. Most likely we would bury some of them later. The Japs grinned! Fires were lit for boiling the pool water and cooking the maggot infested rice. A portion of this and a small piece of dried fish was our meal for the day, washed down with boiled brown pool water.

Our bodies ached and our minds were numb as we crouched around the fires which were kept burning to keep wild animals at bay. No one spoke. What was there to talk about? Each man was cocooned within his own thoughts. They were a comfort, your own thoughts. The night was black now.

The jungle canopy had closed in over us. I realised that further marching the following day would decimate our numbers. Was that the plan, perhaps? A chill ran down my spine. For the first time in my life I knew total misery. I felt alone and very frightened.

Then I became aware of a voice mingling with the many sounds of the night jungle. At first softly, haltingly, then louder, more certain, singing *'Ave Maria'* in a clear tenor voice. The jungle sounds around us subsided one by one as if the night creatures were also listening. The voice was now singing jubilant and triumphant. It was a moment of awe and wonder. The voice filled our hearts and minds as it rose into the silent blackness above us. I knew then that this magic moment would sustain me in the future, whatever situation I would find myself in.

Faces lifted, tears glistening in the fire's glow. Men struggled to their feet, some helped by their comrades. It seemed an impulsive gesture of defiance, as if to say, 'We cannot be beaten.' Were they feeling the same as I was? Were they also ashamed of their earlier misgivings? I believed they were. A glow of pride rose inside me. A pride of belonging. Also a feeling of victory: victory of the human spirit over adversity. Both Japanese soldiers eyed us with bewilderment and suspicion, rifles at the ready. Their eyes darted around the group of quiet men. Men with haggard faces, damp rags hanging from their bones. We were no threat to their wellbeing, yet their eyes showed fear. Fear of something they could not understand. I felt pity for them, then. As the voice softly re-mingled with the returning jungle sounds, the Japanese soldier suddenly snapped, shouting, *'kurra, kurra'*, threatening everyone in sight with the glistening, menacing bayonet.

As he approached me, I smiled. It sent him into a rage. After all, how do you fight a smile? The rifle butt thudded into my body, sending me crashing to the ground. I looked up into his face, now grinning, fury spent, the ridiculously large bayonet aimed at my throat! After a short while, the Jap ambled away, kicking the ground as he went, mumbling to himself. My mates hauled me back onto my feet, their eyes tearful with suppressed anger. I realised, then, that my chest was throbbing with pain. 'No sense of humour, these bastards', someone murmured. I smiled. How right he was.

Constructing the Railway: Cutting at Chungkai Camp. Post War Photo

Several major rock-cuttings were required in building the Thai-Burma Railway. They were mainly cut by POW labour using steel a bar and sledgehammer. Occasionally explosives were used, often with inadequate warning. A similar cutting further north near Kanyu and Kinsayok Camps was christened 'Hell-fire Corner', a First World War reference because the night shift worked by the light of bamboo bonfires - a very fair representation of Hell. - G S Gimson

COMPENSATION
JB

I claim for the loss of the three best things in life:
The companionship of children and of dogs,
And the solace and peace of a garden.

What can you give me in place of the sound of children's laughter,
The sight of their prettiness and grace?
What can you offer me in exchange for the loyalty of my dog
And the innocence in his eyes?
And what in the stead of the place where these things belong -
My garden?

My garden where the sunshine that comes
And the rain that falls
Is mine.
Where the trees and the flowers
Have been given to me under God's law
According as I, and those before me,
Have sown.

Where through the long summer days I can watch the white clouds drifting
High above the elms,
Until at last the long shadows stretching across the grass
Mingle with the on-coming darkness,
And kindly night brings me the stars
To wonder at.

I will have nothing from you but my freedom
So that I can find these things
Again.

(From *Within*, the magazine of No 10 Hut, Argyle Street Internment Camp,
Hong Kong 1942)

PART IV
Mergui and Borneo

THE ROAD TO MERGUI

Narrated by Albert Edward George Raven, 18th Division, Royal Corps of Signals

To the ordinary man in the street the sad history of Far Eastern Prisoners of War brings to mind the famous Railway of Death - and rightly so. It was a supreme tragedy in which thousands of lives were lost under conditions of utter tyranny and suffering. The building of the Mergui Road in 1945 was much smaller in comparison but an even greater tragedy. Its cast of a thousand were all seasoned veterans of The Railway; they had all taken their share in that first tragedy. They were tired; they were not fit. Few men returned from the Mergui Road. Some were luckily evacuated in July. Hundreds died. The remaining few were rescued by Allied troops after the cessation of hostilities.

The droning noise in my ears was persistent and grew louder and louder until I was forced to open my eyes. My head was spinning and my ears were buzzing; my lips were swollen and cracked and my throat was dry. I was soaked in sweat. The sores on my arms and legs had dried and crusted and my groin and armpits were swollen with poison. My fingers cracked as I tried to clench my fists.

'He's waking!' I looked up into the face of the Medical Officer kneeling by my side. He spoke to an orderly. This then had been the droning noise that had awakened me. 'How do you feel?' he asked. As I opened my mouth to reply, a sharp pain ripped at the corners of my mouth. The sores had split. The orderly bathed my lips with water and I drank greedily. I tried again, but this time could only manage to croak. Finally I managed to mumble something sounding like 'not too bad'. He nodded and turned to the orderly and through the haze I heard snatches of conversation: '... spinal malaria ... malnutrition, septicaemia, beriberi ...' I heard no more. I was safe! I was alive and that was the only thing that mattered to me. I had come back to Nakom Paton from the hell and nightmare of the Mergui Road.

Three months previously I had left Nakom Paton with a party of a thousand 'light sick' for a camp down the Kra Isthmus. The Japanese had specially requested a party of 'light sick' for an easy job. Good food, light work and plenty of relaxation were promised. We were glad to go. Nakom Paton was a hospital camp and the whole atmosphere fast became irksome to men recovering from illnesses. Despite its nest appearance it was a grimly dangerous camp for morale.

We should however have known better than to look forward to this 'easy job'! Three years of captivity should have taught us the bitter lesson of believing Japanese statements. Rumours of Allied successes on all fronts had apparently taken the edge off our memories of what had happened during those three bitter years. We actually thought that the Japanese were relenting in the face of defeat. How mistaken we were!

We left Nakom Paton by train on 3rd April 1945 and arrived at Pretchup Kirikan in southern Siam early the following day. We were fairly contented as rumour had it that we were going to erect a new camp for ourselves. We learned the truth at Kirikan. The Japanese had been constructing a road across the Kra Isthmus connecting Kirikan in the Gulf of Siam with Mergui in the Bay of Bengal in Burma. The road was being literally hacked out of the virgin jungle, up over the rocks in the Bilauk Tauno mountain range, before falling into the coastal plain and on to Mergui. Sections of the road had been completed by native labour. Our task was to join up the various sections and finally link up with the Mergui end. There were no natives left on the road - they had either died or run away.

Camps had been established at intervals along the road and having been split into parties we were to march to our various camps. I was in the last party and our task would be to join up the road at its highest point: an eighty-kilometre march in four days. Vainly we protested. The Japs brushed our protests aside. Again we protested. Then followed the usual familiar pattern of events. The Japs cajoled; they promised us everything - food, tobacco and rest. They threatened, they screamed, they swore. Finally came the inevitable platoon of infantry to face us, rifles raised. We knew that we had gone as far as we dared. We gave in, still protesting.

Within an hour we were on our way through the jungle. The march was four days of torture. The atmosphere was humid and the tropical sun beat down mercilessly. Leeches abounded, clinging to our legs and sucking the little blood remaining in our bodies. Such clothing and footwear as we possessed became sodden with sweat. We stripped, took off our footwear and walked barefoot through the dust, mud, rocks and thorns, clad only in our loincloths. Allied planes zoomed over the jungle road at frequent intervals sending us crashing into the undergrowth to emerge bruised, scratched and badly shaken. These planes were armed with cannon.

Water was precious. We were allowed one filling a day in our containers. If we were fortunate enough to come across a stream we jumped in eagerly, ignoring the guards. Dirty water? Who cared? We were past caring. Each night we staggered into a broken down bamboo staging camp sited by a stream. Here in the darkness we would bathe, have a meal of rice and dried fish and bed down for the night.

The camps were infested with bugs and mosquitoes with an ever-present stench. Each night became an eternal battle between the mosquitoes, the bugs and our weary bodies. Each day's march was the same. We rose before dawn: a mess tin of rice for breakfast and a refill for the journey. We carried our sick from camp to camp and at each camp we picked up further things to carry. We picked up our supply of shovels, axes and *chunkols*. We picked up our rice supply in two-hundredweight sacks together with our supplies of dried fruit and seaweed. At our last camp we even picked up our cooking equipment. We were ill-equipped to face this task. Three years of harsh and bitter treatment had tried us sorely and our bodies were weak through disease and lack of proper food.

The last day's march for our party bound for the top camp was even worse than those preceding. We turned off the road through a narrow jungle track. Ragged, unkempt, haggard and weary, we made our way slowly through the undergrowth. The track was uphill and slipping: the undergrowth thick and wet. The tall trees, pushing upwards for light and air above the undergrowth, closed in on us, enveloping the whole atmosphere in a gloomy world of semi-darkness. We were now high up the slopes of the mountains, and the effects of the constant marching was taking its inevitable toll. Many collapsed and needed to be carried on improvised stretchers; others tottered or staggered, always helped along by their comrades, and inevitably the whole burden of carrying the equipment fell on those of us who were comparatively fit. Now and again came the shout of '*Yazume*' from our guards and wearily we would sink to the ground. To speak was an effort.

Late that afternoon we reached our camp. In a small jungle clearing by the side of a narrow shallow stream stood two broken down bamboo huts, their *attap* roofs a mass of holes. In many places the bamboo sleeping platforms had broken down and collapsed and lay on the floor in a tangled heap. It was more foul and primitive than any camp I had ever seen. Its mud floors were littered with filth and a horrible stench permeated the atmosphere.

A feeling of fear and foreboding gripped me. Both ahead and behind us lay the dense jungle. No further supplies of food would reach us until the road was through from the base at Kirikan and we would never leave this camp until we had flung the road over the mountains towards Mergui. We were trapped high above the world in this seemingly impenetrable jungle and the only means of exit rested entirely on the efforts that could be extracted from our weak and weary bodies. The beginnings of the awful truth behind this project had been nagging at my thoughts all through the march and then it flashed. This was to be a one way road and not, as we thought, a supply road for the Japanese in Burma!

We had been prisoners for so long and our senses were so dulled that it hardly seemed feasible that the Japanese offensive in Burma could be so quickly turned into a retreat. The Japanese were retreating headlong before the victorious Allied Armies and this road was to be an avenue of escape. Hence the urgency of this task and the need for its completion before the monsoon season in July.

We started our task the following day, pushing steadily forward towards Tenasserim. We felled trees, removed clumps of tough bamboo, shifted great boulders and generally levelled a surface of roughly twenty feet wide. Our tools were bad, our picks too light. The axes and saws had long since lost their keen edge. We had no time to spare for proper care and maintenance of these tools and they became daily more dilapidated, thus increasing our difficulties. We dug, picked and shovelled. We toiled from dawn to long after darkness, returning to camp only when the Japanese were satisfied that we were physically incapable of further work for the day.

The heat of the day was stifling and the perspiration dried on our bodies in a fine layer of salt. This salt attracted swarms of wasps buzzing angrily around our weary bodies. Leeches clung to our legs and toes, dropping off only when their bloated bodies could draw no more blood. At night we toiled by the light of naphtha flares. Our guards, mostly Japanese, were less harsh in their treatment of us than those of the Railway. Gone was the sadistic outbreak of violence, the bashings and kickings; but they were never lenient.

As we toiled on through April into May and June we were steadily getting nearer to our goal. Each morning took us further away from camp to commence our task. Every night at ten, sometimes midnight or even early morning, we trod our weary way back to camp. The food, consisting of rice and seaweed stew, sometimes dried fish, was appalling. The accumulation of these wretched conditions inevitably took its toll. Each day fewer men paraded for work and each day the few fit men had to do the full quota for the whole party. Malaria, septicaemia, beriberi and malnutrition took their heavy toll and our death roll mounted slowly. Our food supplies dwindled and even rice became scarce. Again and again we appealed to the Japanese, only to meet with the same blunt answer, 'Road finish, lorry bring food'. Thus the lives of all rested on the few remaining fit and their chances of putting through the road before the monsoons.

We finished the road in July and took a well-earned rest, waiting for the lorries to come from Kirikan with food. But it was too late. The monsoons broke and the top slopes of the road became a slipping, sliding quagmire through which no mechanical transport could run. The lorries came only as far as the halfway stage and if we wanted food we would have to walk down and carry it back. We were also informed that none of us was going back even though the road was completed. We were to stay on and maintain the road during the rainy season, thus ensuring it would be kept in good repair.

We were stunned by this awful news. We somehow felt then that for us the end would not be long delayed. No food, the greater part of our camp down with malaria, no quinine, no drugs, and the monsoons upon us. Utterly exhausted, we were in no condition to offer any resistance to the forces ranged against us. England's green and pleasant land was a fast fading dream.

Now I was sick. After working the whole of the time on the road I had finally succumbed. Attack after attack of malaria had weakened my resistance. I strove desperately to shake off this vile fever but supplies of quinine were inadequate. My ankles swelled with beriberi; my tongue was blistered and raw, and the jungle sores on my arms and legs had turned septic. Weak, weary and dispirited, my mind was growing dull with the eternal misery and hopelessness. Then to me and a few others came a challenge - a challenge to fight for very life itself.

I do not know where the instructions came from: Nakom Paton may have heard of our plight or the Japanese may have suddenly become afraid of the situation which was swiftly getting out of hand and rushing headlong towards its inevitable end. The sick men who could walk paraded before the Japanese *Gunso*. I managed somehow to join them, and stood swaying on my feet in the burning sun with my blanket around my shoulders. Slowly he passed in front of us, muttering and nodding. He looked at me. 'You malaria - *Ka*?' I nodded. 'You *taxan* malaria - *Ka*?' I nodded again then replied, '*Taxan* malaria, *go-ju* times.' 'You go Kirikan,' he said. 'Malaria no *goodena*.' He passed on down the line and picked out about twenty men. We were to go back down the road to Kirikan - on foot.

This was our only chance and I for one was determined to make it if I had to crawl there. So we started off back down the road. Some walked by themselves. Others, myself included, walked in pairs or groups, helping each other along. We took one guard. The marks of suffering and agony showed in each and every one of us: gaunt, haggard and unshaven; our hair hanging down to our shoulders; the bones in our faces, ribs and thighs standing out as terrible evidence of the malnutrition. Slowly but steadily we pushed on towards the next camp which we somehow reached by nightfall. Here we found that conditions were much the same and we left the following morning taking with us a further quota of walking sick.

That night we staggered into the halfway camp to come across the most distressing sight I have ever witnessed. It was as if one had entered a graveyard. The *attap*-roofed huts, once lofty, through wind and general neglect had become dilapidated. Many of the bamboo sleeping platforms had collapsed and now lay on the ground in a mass of dusty bamboo and *attap*. Many preferred to sleep in the open. Virtually the whole camp was sick, lying there staring into space. A few were able to make their way slowly to the cookhouse. It was a camp of walking dead. Here lay the results of the last mad and sadistic acts of the Japanese: the final tragedy in the drama that had lasted for three and a half years. These men were too sick to be transported to base.

I made my way slowly down the steps to the stream and lay down full length in the shallow water. I was tired and weary and I could feel the heaviness and languor slowly creeping over me, and it was evident that another bout of malaria was on its way. My legs and arms were stiff with the jungle sores and it was an effort to move my fingers. I dried myself in the loincloth, slipped on my tattered shorts and made my way wearily back to the camp area. My head was aching and my ears buzzing and I began to shiver. Wrapping my blanket around me, I lay down before the huge fire that was burning in the area to sink into a fitful sleep.

Dawn came and with it transportation to take us to Kirikan. I staggered to my feet to join the party and by an effort of grim determination I managed to crawl the twenty yards or so to the truck. Someone lifted me aboard and I sank into a corner of the lorry, oblivious to what was happening around me. Vaguely I remembered the bumps and the swaying and the frequent stops before we finally arrived at Kirikan. Here we rested by the side of the railway track for our train to take us to Nakom Paton. The rest partially revived me and although the fever was still with me I began to take notice of events around me.

Kirikan had changed, its hive of activity replaced by an air of desolation. Frequent air strikes by Allied aircraft had left a trail of destruction. Buildings had been flattened and the ground was pockmarked with craters. A few smiling Siamese came over and chatted to us in the universally used pidgin English, completely ignoring our guard. They brought us coffee, bananas and tobacco and we accepted gratefully. They told us the news of the end of the war in Europe and the headlong flight of the Japanese in Burma.

We entrained that evening, slowly making our way to Ratburi. Allied planes were sweeping the skies almost continuously. Many times we stopped and took to the paddy, running helter-skelter away from the train which presented a sitting target. Fate was with us and we wended our way slowly towards Ratburi and into a scene of utter chaos. The town had been blanket bombed the previous day. The railway track was the focal point of utter wreckage. The bombers had scored a direct hit on a troop train. Pieces of carriages and metal lay everywhere and a gaping hole presented what had once been the station. A span of the giant steel bridge that carried the railway over the river was missing, and hastily erected to bridge the gap was a crazy swaying narrow bamboo construction. We had to cross that bridge on foot.

By now I was again shivering with a further attack of fever. I accepted a mouthful of rice and a drink of water and immediately brought the lot up. I was beginning to get delirious and I could not coordinate the thoughts of my brain with the movements of my limbs. We slowly made our way towards the bridge, climbing over the debris as we went. I put my foot on that swaying bamboo catwalk and immediately fell on my hands and knees and crawled over. Through the oblivion of my mind one thought prevailed. I got over and collapsed in a heap on the grass verge.

The remainder of that journey was a haze. We passed through the old staging area of Bampong where so many of us had camped when we first came to Thailand. We stopped at Non Pladuk, scene of the disastrous bombing by Allied planes early in 1945 where so many were killed. I remember being propped up on the parade ground at Nakom Paton.

I awoke in hospital two days later. I was alive! I had beaten the combination of the Japanese and spinal malaria. The nightmare of the Mergui Road was over.

BORNEO DEATH MARCH
Major Archie Black

The War Cemetery at Labuan was specially constructed to receive graves from Sandaken which was evacuated due to flooding, and from other sites all over Borneo. One of the 2,115 unknown buried there could be Bombardier Tom Tadman of the Lanarkshire Yeomanry. After forty years of painstaking research at their own expense Tom's family was able to get very close to his last movements. Tom and five other comrades from 155 Regiment sailed to Kuching on the infamous *De Klerk* on 26th March 1943 with 500 British and 500 Australian POWs. The 500 British troops were sent to Jesselton. (For convenience the names of locations will be those in use when the area was British Borneo). The Australians were sent to Sandaken to join other POWs already there, including 750 British servicemen. Tom's family believes he then went to one of the smaller camps, possibly Kota Belu, and met his death later during a forced march back to Jesselton.

In 1945, with the war going against them, the Japanese started moving POWs to other camps in north Borneo, away from the advancing Allied troops. The following is a modified edition of the story concerning the evacuation of Sandaken to be included in the forthcoming work by Doctor J Pritchard on Japanese atrocities during World War II.

Colonel Sugo, Commander of all Allied POWs in Borneo, ordered the movement of POWs from Sandaken to Ranau, 150 miles further north, and from other smaller camps to new locations. This order was given against the background of a Japanese High Command Order: 'If Allied troops land on Japanese held territory, the prisoners of war are to be exterminated by whatever means possible.' What followed is a story of terrible degradation and barbaric depravity imposed by a sadistic and pitiless enemy on helpless POWs. At Sandaken, the Camp Commandant, the six-foot Captain Hoshijima, acted with alacrity on the plan to exterminate POWs. Their bodies and spirits had to be broken. There was the daily sickening spectacle of severe beatings, causing the sick-rate to rise and followed by the inevitable increased number of deaths - all this against demands for larger work parties.

The majority of POWs at Sandaken were marched off in two large groups. Although the first group of 470 men left on 28th January and the second party of 537 three months later, the order of march followed the same pattern. It was calculated to inflict maximum casualties en route. Each marching group was divided into smaller parties of fifty, guarded by about twenty to thirty armed soldiers which left little opportunity for escape. Their destination was Ranau, about 150 miles to the north, along jungle tracks, through knee-deep swamps and over a mountain ridge. As they stumbled along, they were grotesque images of their former selves due to malnutrition, dysentery, beriberi and constant maltreatment.

When the order was given to march, the starving, crippled and sick POWs set off across north Borneo. None was spared: they had to march. When dying and exhausted men fell out they were shot, bayoneted or beaten to death by the Japanese guards who drove the others on, leaving the bodies to rot where they lay. One morning, a mile from the Muanad River crossing, seventy-three men who were unable to continue were callously machine-gunned to death. Despite several desperate attempts to escape, only one man, an Australian, Bombardier Braithwaite, was successful. The others were shot.

The casualty figures are the final censure of this catalogue of suffering, despair and death. When the survivors of the second party reached Ranau on 25th June they were met by six skeletal figures: all that remained of the 470 men who had left Sandaken five months previously. The second party had suffered grievous losses also. Only 183 reached Ranau. Two Australians had made a successful escape but behind them, along jungle tracks in swampy land and on the steep slopes of Maitland Range, were scattered the remains of 350 men. Dreadful treatment was meted out to two POWs who were caught after a failed escape attempt. The survivor was tied naked to a post outside the guardroom and hung there for several days being beaten by every passing Japanese soldier before he also died.

Dr Picone of the Australian Army Medical Corps determined someone must make an escape and tell the authorities about these terrible events. Plans were laid and four men, Private Botterill and Bombardier Moxham, survivors from the first group, and Privates Short and Anderson from the second group were selected. Private Anderson did not survive but the others did.

Natives at Ranau described the prisoners in the last days of captivity: men like skeletons clad in loincloth rags with long beards whose heads moved from side to side as they walked. They were dying of exhaustion, malnutrition, disease and unimaginable filth. On the night of 28th July, a Formosan guard, Takahara, a conscripted Christian who had befriended an Australian Warrant Officer W Sticpewich, warned him that all men were to be killed. With Driver A Reither, Sticpewich made his escape that night. In the hut behind him were thirty-two men who were barely alive. He was convinced eight would die before morning. Reither died of dysentery during the escape but Sticpewich was guided to an Australian Reconnaissance

Division by friendly natives on 24th August. A message was immediately radioed to GHQ to speed up the relief of POW camps.

Warrant Officer Sticpewich remained in the Army and assisted in the identification and interrogation of Japanese soldiers responsible for these atrocities. He also assisted the Australian War Graves Commission in recovering the remains of POWs who had died along that track.

There were no survivors from those who had remained at Sandaken. It is known, possibly from locally employed natives, that a third group of seventy-five men was marched away and never heard of again: twenty-three were taken out to the aerodrome and massacred. The end of the 400 stretcher cases left in the open while their 'hospital' huts were burned to the ground as the second group left for Ranau, can only be imagined.

Colonel Suga committed suicide at Labuan by cutting his throat. Captain Takuo Takakuwa, Camp Commandant at Sandaken, who told the War Crimes Tribunal that, 'On 1st August 1945, I issued orders that all POWs were to be killed, based on the necessity of war operations,' was later hanged along with another camp commandant, Captain Susumu Hoshijima.

The story of the Borneo Death Marches featured in the Daily Mail about May 1945 under a banner headline 'The Green Hell Of Borneo'. A 'D Notice' was quickly served on the paper as it was deemed not to be in the public interest. The story was repeated on 13th November of the same year, then after that - nothing! There were no British survivors from north Borneo, no one to relate their experiences. Perhaps without the 'human interest' angle it could not compete with the many other stories of atrocities told by survivors from other areas in the Far East.

In July 1995 the Australian Government organised the 50th Anniversary Ceremony by paying homage at Memorials and Gardens of Remembrance at Sandaken and Ranau with a final Service at Labuan War Cemetery. Len and Dorothy Tadman, the only persons present from the UK, received a warm welcome from Mr Bruce Ruxton OBE, President of the Returned Servicemen's League. He immediately arranged transport for them for the remainder of their visit. It was a gesture fully appreciated as they had brought with them five wreaths and one hundred poppies for distribution amongst the five sites. They also had a tape of the Pipes and Drums of the Black Watch to be played in memory of British dead. The Australian Government ensured that those evil massacres were not forgotten and due honour was accorded to the victims of one of the worst atrocities against Allied POWs in World War II.

JAP GERM WARFARE

Japan had consistently followed a policy of imperial expansion and had refused to join international moves towards the limitation of arms. As early as 1925 Japan had refused to approve a treaty proposed by a Geneva Convention governing wartime conduct which would ban biological weapons.

In 1932, in pursuance of its policy of imperialism, Japanese troops invaded Manchuria and in the same year Shiro Ishii, a physician, began preliminary experiments in germ warfare, forming Unit 731, a biological-warfare unit, in 1932. The unit was disguised as a water purification farm and consisted of a huge compound outside the city of Harbin. Tens of thousands of test subjects, including Allied prisoners of war, died eventually of bubonic plague, cholera, anthrax and other diseases.

After the surrender, Japanese troops destroyed the headquarters of Unit 731, killing off the remaining prisoners to cover up their experimentation. Ishii and other Unit 731 leaders were given immunity, on the instructions of General McArthur, from war-crimes prosecution on condition that they work for the Allies. Subsequently a congressional subcommittee held a one-day hearing aimed at determining whether US prisoners of war in Manchuria were victims of germ warfare experimentation but reached no conclusion.

PART V
Ships and Mines

Lisbon Maru

SINKING OF THE LISBON MARU

Lieutenant G W Hamilton, 2nd Battalion, The Royal Scots

The second draft of prisoners of war to be sent from Hong Kong to Japan, a total of 1,816, was embarked on *SS Lisbon Maru* on 25th September 1942 under the command of Lieutenant Wada. The *Lisbon Maru* was not marked in any way to indicate that she carried prisoners of war, and was in every way similar to an ordinary armed transport.

Officers and other ranks were all accommodated in three holds: the 2nd Battalion The Royal Scots; the 1st Battalion the Middlesex Regiment; the Royal Artillery and some small units. There was not quite enough room for all men to lie down at the same time. Food was adequate according to prisoner-of-war standards: rice and tea in the morning; rice, a quarter of a tin of bully beef and a spoonful of vegetables in the evening. Water for drinking was limited but adequate; water for washing was non-existent. The men were allowed on deck for fresh air at prescribed periods. There were also some 2,000 Japanese troops on board.

At 0700 hours on 1st October 1942 the ship was struck by a torpedo and came to a halt. None of the prisoners was hurt by the explosion. The few men who were on deck were immediately sent into the hold and sentries placed to prevent exit. In the holds, although no one knew if or when the ship would sink, the troops remained perfectly calm. The after-gun, a three-inch approximately, was fired several times, and some time later Japanese planes appeared and various explosions were heard.

As there were no latrines in the holds, requests were made to use the latrines on deck or to provide receptacles. Both requests were refused. About fourteen hours later and without food the Japanese began to batten down the hatches above us. Lieutenant-Colonel Stewart, the senior British officer on board, requested that at least one baulk of timber be left for air, but the request was refused. All the hatches were closed, tarpaulins were thrown over the top, and the whole lot was roped down. There was no other means of exit from the hold, and as there was no inlet of air, conditions became rapidly worse. The men remained perfectly calm.

Hold No 3 was making water and the pumps had to be manned. Men working the pumps rapidly lost consciousness owing to the extreme heat and the lack of air. A man could do about six strokes on the pump before fainting. In our hold (No 2), although air conditions were similar, we could remain conscious by lying flat and doing nothing. Hold No 1 reported that two men had died. At intervals during the day and night Lieutenant Potter of the St

John's Ambulance Brigade who was acting as our interpreter, requested air, water, or an interview with Lieutenant Wada. All were refused. During the day a ship came alongside and took off the Japanese soldiers.

By dawn on 2nd October, twenty-four hours after the torpedoing, the air in the holds was dangerously foul. A few hours after dawn the ship gave a lurch, and it became evident that she was going to sink. Lieutenant-Colonel Stewart authorised a small party to try to break out of the hold with a view to asking the Japanese to give us a sporting chance to swim. On his order, some men pushed their knives between the baulks of timber above them, cut the ropes, slit the canvas tarpaulin, and pushed up one of the timbers. Through the opening, Lieutenant Howell, Lieutenant Potter and one or two others, climbed on to the deck and walked slowly towards the bridge, asking in Japanese for an interview with the captain. The Japanese opened fire, wounding Lieutenant Potter who subsequently died. The others returned to the hold and reported to Lieutenant-Colonel Stewart that the ship was evidently about to sink. A moment later the Japanese fired a couple of times into the hold. Then the ship gave another lurch and sank by the stern, water pouring into our hold through the hole in the hatch. The stern landed on a sandbank, while the bow and a third of the ship's length remained sticking out of the water for about an hour.

The men stationed at the hatch now cut the ropes and canvas and forced up the baulks of timber, while the remainder formed into queues and poured up from the hold. Hold No 1 and No 3 broke out at the same time, but many of the men in No 3 hold, nearest the stern, were trapped by the water and drowned. As we got out, the Japanese opened fire from one of the ships standing by and continued to fire at the men after they had plunged over the side into the water.

About five miles away were some islands towards which a swift current was running but they appeared to be rocky and dangerous. About four Japanese ships were standing by, but appeared equally inhospitable. At first the Japanese refused to pick anyone out of the water. Ropes were dangled over the side, but the men who tried to climb them were kicked back into the water. Later the Japanese policy changed and they began to pick men up. Some men reached the islands, but many were lost on the rocky coast. Others were picked up by Chinese junks and sampans from the islands. These Chinese treated the men with great kindness, giving them food and clothing and looking after them until the Japanese landing party came to recover them.

Many men were naked, and all suffered greatly from the cold as we were kept on deck under a tarpaulin which leaked badly. Food consisted of four hard-tack biscuits and two small cups of watered milk per day, with a bowl of soup on the third day. The cold and exposure were undoubtedly responsible for the large amount of disease which later broke out. By 5th October all officers and men were assembled on the dock at Shanghai, where roll call was taken. From an original total of 1,816 men, 970 answered their names, leaving 846 men missing. Some half-dozen had managed to escape with the aid of the Chinese.

Those who arrived in Japan were put to work in mines and factories. About 200 died, most of them during the first winter, from dysentery, diarrhoea, diphtheria, pneumonia and malnutrition.

It appeared to us that the Japanese had intended to drown all British personnel and would then say that the ship sank instantaneously. That fifty per cent of the men did escape was due to the fact that the stern of the ship landed on a sandbank, that the islands and Chinese were near, and that a strong tide was flowing towards the islands. It was only after the Japanese had seen that large numbers of men were already being picked up by the Chinese that they decided to pick up the remainder. It might be added that they could have saved every man by taking the prisoners of war off the ship when they transferred the Japanese soldiers to another ship.

SNAPSHOT

By July 1945, the food shortage in the Andaman Islands was serious and the Japanese committed several atrocities on the civilian population. Three hundred 'useless mouths': the aged and infirm; women and children; and all those who were not employed by the Japanese and therefore had no ration cards, were taken from their houses, stripped of their possessions and embarked on three ships. Off Havelock Island, a jungle-covered uninhabited island off the north-east coast of South Andaman, the Japanese forced them into the water, to wade ashore. By 21st September 1945, only eleven were still alive. Allied investigators found the bones and skulls of 180 men, women and children on the islands and the remains of many others in the sand below high water mark. On 13th August (two days before the Jap surrender) some 700 more men, women and children were taken to the island of Taimulgi where they were all shot by a firing party of Japanese soldiers. The bodies were thrown into mass graves and covered with earth. However, the officer in charge was ordered by Tokyo to dig up the bodies and burn them. If asked, he was to say that they had been taken safely to Port Campbell and released.

THE HELL-SHIP THAT SAILED FROM KOWLOON
'A Diehard'

How many are left that remember
The hell-ship that sailed from Kowloon?
How many boys have grown into men?
How many have died far too soon?

She sailed from Hong Kong on a fine autumn day
Full of prisoners en route for Nippon
Bound for the land which we'd been told
Would welcome the fit and the strong.

Four days out in the China seas,
The weather fair and the water calm,
When a thump from below is felt by all.
The engines stop. Is there cause for alarm?

'Below!' 'Below!' shouts the Jap in charge
And into the holds we are crammed,
Battened down like rats in a trap,
A hell-hole, and we are the damned.

Two days and nights we suffered such fate
With no water, no food and no light.
The air it was foul with our own hot breaths,
We were snared by our own hopeless plight.

We could feel that the ship was sinking
And we knew that our time had run out.
'Break open the hatches!' came the order,
'It's now or never,' echoed the shout.

Up from below like the proverbial rats
We clambered out into the light.
Then the Nips began shooting, the bastards!
Men died with no hope of a fight.

Down the sloping decks into the water -
Thank God it was calm and clear!
We slid and we jumped and we scurried,
Too relieved at release to sense fear.

Strung out in a line just like flotsam
We were carried away on the tide.
Some made it ashore to an island,
Some floated away and were drowned.

One thousand eight hundred and sixteen
POWs were aboard when she sank,
And over a thousand perished
On a Jap ship that was sunk by a Yank!

How many are left to remember?
Time has whittled them down to a few.
Yet we who remain will never forget
That hell-ship the *Lisbon Maru*.

1100 POWs DROWNED

RAF Officer, Aidan Mac Carthy's War
Barry Reed

There were now 10,000 prisoners in the camp. After several months, the camp was split. MacCarthy was marched off to Tan Jon Priok, Batavia's seaport. Then 1,200 Dutch, British and American POWs were crowded onto a cargo ship, sleeping five or six deep on wooden bunks in the ship's hold. Again, many of the POWs died and could not be removed and thrown overboard until nightfall. Diarrhoea was rampant, and the atmosphere was one continuous stench. The hatches were routinely slammed down when air raid or submarine alarms sounded. The prisoners sat terrified in the steaming darkness, expecting a torpedo to strike at any moment. As their convoy steamed up Formosa Strait, it was attacked by American bombers. By the time they reached the Ryukyu Islands, all the accompanying Japanese destroyers had been sunk. On the final night of the voyage, the Japanese mainland twinkled into view. The guards and crew sang and drank themselves into a stupor, some sharing their booze with the prisoners. MacCarthy and his group joined in the singing. At least for now they were safe. 'We sang all the wartime songs that were made so popular by Vera Lynn,' MacCarthy recalled, 'and before being ordered to bed down, for a finale we sang "I'll Be With You In Apple Blossom Time." Then the torpedo struck.'

The torpedo exploded directly underneath MacCarthy, blowing off the ship's keel. The lights went out, and the ship began to sink. MacCarthy grabbed a life jacket and scrambled to the deck. The ship was nose-diving into the ocean with its stern tilting higher and higher. As the vessel made its death plunge, MacCarthy jumped, expecting to be sucked down after it. 'Fortunately, nothing happened,' he later wrote in his journal, 'and I realised that I was not going to die just yet. I began to pray, thanking God for making me a veteran survivor, and asking His help for strength to survive again.' He grasped a small island of wreckage floating by. Cries and screams sounded all around him. He could hear them above the crackle of flames from a burning tanker nearby that had also been hit. 'And all the while,' he recalled, 'the stars shone placidly down on the carnage below them.'

As dawn approached, he could make out floating bodies. They were women and children who had been evacuated from the Philippines, their ship torpedoed about the same time as his. He looked down into the face of one child, staring into its sightless eyes, seeing its mouth forever fixed in an eternal scream.

The temperature of the sea was moderate. Nevertheless, everyone clinging to bits of wreckage became saturated with seawater, and their skins turned a shrivelled grey. They prayed for rescue, even a Japanese rescue. 'We were merely human flotsam on a dawn-stirred sea,' MacCarthy remembered, 'dumbly bobbing up and down, all thought merging into one silent, despairing cry for help.' Finally, after twelve agonising hours in the sea, about twenty of the group were picked up by a Japanese destroyer. Thinking the navy would be more humane, they were rudely surprised when they were systematically beaten up and thrown overboard. Some who had been beaten unconscious were sucked into the revolving screws of the destroyer and disappeared in a red whirlpool. Those surviving secured pieces of wreckage and tried to swim to the Cheju Do Islands, some eighteen miles distant. A passing fishing boat picked up their little armada of despair and then steamed into Nagasaki.

In all, eighty-two survivors stood naked on the dock. They were marched through the streets of Nagasaki, carrying some of their fellow survivors on makeshift litters, others hobbling on sticks. A small sense of elation came over them. Even as they shambled along with the crowds jeering at them, they took it calmly. Some of the Aussies gave a 'V' sign. 'Obviously dangerous,' noted MacCarthy, 'but we had been through so much we were all a little insane.'

SNAPSHOT

At Tenko each night the parade was taken in Japanese and we had to number *'Ichi, ni, san, see, go ...'* The next man couldn't remember the Japanese for 'six' so the count began again with the same result: *'Ichi, ni, san, see, go ...* Silence. *'Conero!'* (you blockhead) shouted the Jap sergeant delivering a face-slap. Again he gave the order, *'Bungo!'* (number). This time things were different: *'Ichi, ni, san, see, go, conero!'*

THE AWU MARU

Southend Focus on POW Affairs No 12

The *Awu Maru* was one of two Jap ships sailing under a guarantee of safe conduct by British and American governments and the Red Cross to carry relief supplies to all Allied POWs and interned civilians. The cunning Japs saw this as a possible means of getting armaments and food to their own troops throughout South East Asia as at this time the Jap merchant fleet had been almost wiped out. Their plan also was to return to Japan important officials and technicians needed for the war effort.

The US Navy delivered over 2000 tons of food and clothing for Allied prisoners of war to a Siberian port. The Japanese ship, the *Hoshi Maru* which departed with the stores on 8th January 1945, reached Shanghai without incident. The *Awu Maru*, a much larger ship with a cargo capacity of 12,000 tons, left soon after. To safeguard their passage, both ships were to have white crosses painted on the hulls, funnels and hatch covers. All US submarine commanders in the Pacific received the clear message LET THE *AWU MARU* PROCEED SAFELY - SHE CARRIES PRISONER OF WAR SUPPLIES.

Unbeknown to the neutral authorities the Japs had loaded many boxes of stolen gold but the US, having broken the codes, knew of this Japanese secret cargo. At Indonesia, she took on a huge tonnage of tin and rubber and many Japanese officials and technicians. On the night of 1st April, the US submarine *Queenfish* made contact at a range of 17,000 yards and her commander, Charles Loughlin, who said he assumed the *Awu Maru* to be a Jap warship, fired a spread of four torpedoes, all of which hit the ship, sinking her. Only one survivor out of 2000 was found, making this one of the worst wartime disasters.

Loughlin was court-martialled, admonished and subsequently promoted to Rear Admiral!

IRUKU COPPER MINES

Syd Brewis

At the POW camp at Iruku in the mountains we worked in the copper mines. The seams in the mines ran vertical unlike UK mines. The mine was owned and operated by the Ishiharo Sangyo Coy who supplied everything to the camp including clothing and food. They also supplied the alloy hard hats which only lasted about a month in the wet areas of the workings due to the acid water dropping on us. All the clothing, rice bowls and work clothes had a company badge on them. The working clothes were made of a sort of sackcloth which we named onion bag tweed.

The camp we were in at first was demolished in a hurricane and after about a week we were moved to another just over the road where the buildings were good. We had electric light when it worked but the accommodation was very overcrowded - about thirty on two tiers in a very small room. We also suffered a small earthquake with a few minor tremors following it. It was quite an experience for those working in the mine at the time seeing the pit props falling. Luckily no one was hurt.

Rations in Iruku were very low although we did get the odd Red Cross parcel: one to about thirty men. On a couple of occasions we were sent out on *Yasume* (rest) day to gather young bracken from the hills to eat. Speaking to a farmer in the Cheviots about this he said it would poison his sheep if they ate it! The camp garden supplied some food: a type of radish and potatoes where we got the tops and the guards got the spuds. These were fertilised by raw sewage from the camp latrines.

After the war ended we built a memorial to sixteen of the lads who died at Iruku. Some were killed in mine accidents. The memorial has been looked after since we left and fresh flowers placed on it daily by the people of the village.

Excerpts from
BANZAI YOU BASTARDS
Jack Edwards OBE, Montrose and Hong Kong

Kinkaseki was one of the worst prison camps in the Far East ... we were issued black cardboard helmets, canvas shoes, a threadbare short-sleeved green shirt and shorts - these were to be our 'mining clothes' ... we marched up about 250 steps to the brow of the hill (above the camp) and in the distance below us we could see the mine-head - we had to clamber all the way down on a very rough path with stone steps ... we were marched to the mine entrance and forced to stop at a small Japanese shrine to pray for our safety in the mine ... then into the mine ... for forty-five minutes we trudged on and then turning off to the left, climbed down very rough steps under a low ceiling for several levels ... the warm air hit us ... water dripped down, quite warm ... down we went, getting hotter and hotter ... there were cries of pain all around as we caught our backs or arms on the jagged walls and low ceiling ... I thought we were descending into hell ...

...after descending nearly 800 steps, we were given our tools - a *chunkel* and a two-handled bamboo basket ... our task was to scrape the ore into the basket and then carry it to the trolley (ore cart) which we called bogies and then to push the full trolley to the cage ... at lunchtime we would return to the rest area to eat our *bento* - only to find it alive with cockroaches.

The slave labour underground went on year after year in conditions of extreme danger. We were subjected to savage floggings if weakness or illness prevented us from digging the required quota of copper ore. For war crimes investigations in January 1946, the only copy of the secret order from the Japanese High Command to massacre all POWs and leave no traces - applicable to all camps in the Far East - was found at Kinkaseki. This order, known only to a select, secret committee of six, including myself, hung over us for nearly a year before the A-bombs and liberation by US Marines.

SNAPSHOT

There were these three wee grandfather-types chattering away nineteen to the dozen in this hotel lobby in Xian, north west China last year.

'You looked like you'd all just come out of the same mould, like the Terracotta warriors, only smaller,' said the wife.

There was plenty to chat about. Glyn from Glouchester had been navigator on transport planes flying out of India during the war.

'Ever get over Thailand?' asked Tom.

'Nope, never crossed the Irrawady. But Donald here, was navigator of Liberators flying out of Calcutta. He did some bombing out your way.'

'Which camp were you in?' asked Donald from Haddington. 'Nonpladuk? O Christ!'

'I went back with my wife to Nonpladuk some years ago,' said Donald, and she said, "What were you doing wasting your time on a wee place like this?" But of course it was a lot bigger and busier in those days.'

'Well we knew you were there but our mission was to get the rail marshalling yards and we did our best to miss you. You'd obviously been put there as a human shield. That would be January '45.'

'I think it was December '44,' I said. 'First time we'd seen our own planes close up. One stick fell across the camp and from memory it was ninety-seven of our chaps bought it. Would have been fewer but a lot were standing up cheering you instead of getting into the trenches.'

PART VI
Pests and Pets

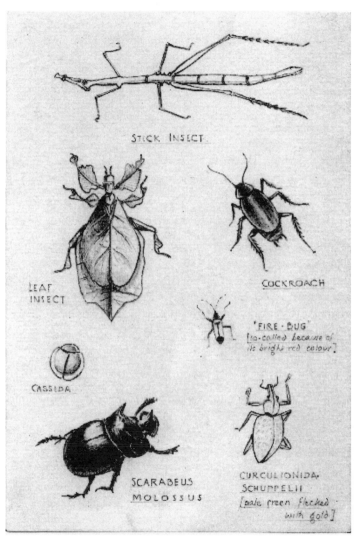

Typical Insects

Most of these insects would not have disturbed the POWs. Bed bugs, cockroaches, lice, and in the animal world, rats and scorpions, were the major pests. - G S Gimson

PESTS AND PETS
A J D Allison

Prisoner of War camps are not generally associated with the study of insect and animal life, but for those prisoners interested, the opportunities were there in their millions. Unfortunately the variety was not of our own choosing, and the discomfort they caused quickly dampened any enthusiasm to study their habits.

Judging by the number of fleas which greeted us on our arrival at Jinsen (now Inchon) Camp, Korea, it seemed as if there had been a worldwide flea migration to this one spot. Quite literally they hopped and crawled over us in their thousands. As we had arrived 'flealess ' from Singapore, the plague must have been a local brand, probably stored up in the Japanese blankets issued to us on arrival. Army blankets in Japan apparently are never washed, and ownership changes frequently as blankets are handed in and reissued at the different seasons of the year. However, we were not in a position to be fussy. Korean winters are bitterly cold, and it was a case of either accepting the blankets - and the fleas - or freezing to death. We chose the fleas!

Having accepted a few thousand Japanese fleas, our next task was to get rid of them. Swatting, we soon found, was a waste of time. The fleas seemed to have an Indiarubber-like power of resistance even to a direct hit. Catching them alive and breaking their backs between our thumbnails was the only effective way of administering certain death. Flea-catching became an automatic occupation at all hours of the day, even at meal times and during casual conversation, but experience soon taught us that the best hunting time was the early morning. As we slept on the floor, each prisoner usually collected two or three dozen casual guests in his blanket during the night, and by morning the fleas, having dined well, were comfortably warm and drowsy. Many were still sufficiently alert to escape as we pulled our blankets off, but each of us generally managed to average about a dozen victims per morning. An expert recorded twenty-seven one morning.

A few of us later introduced the 'flea-bag' simply by sewing our blankets into a bag. In the mornings we wriggled carefully out, closed the mouth of our 'bag,' and shook the contents into a pail of water. This method was more thorough, although the excitement of the morning flea hunt was missed.

Our onslaught made little impression however, and eventually we resorted to a *blitzkrieg*. For several successive days the contents of all huts were taken out into the sunshine while the interiors were sluiced down with buckets of water on a lavish scale. The Japanese were both surprised and interested in the behaviour of the eccentric British. Apparently the flea is regarded as an inevitable part of Japanese army life.

After this campaign we learned to tolerate fleas in small quantities, but other insects encountered were much more unpopular. Bugs and lice we loathed. After our experience of all these insects aboard the *Fukkai Maru* which transported us from Singapore to Korea, we were thankful to find that they seldom troubled us in Korea, possibly as a result of the rigorous climate.

In our early days at Changi Camp, Singapore, we were continually fighting a losing battle against bugs. Their numbers were increasing daily, but after some months a prisoner miraculously produced a blow-lamp, seemingly the only effective destructive weapon with bugs, and the bug army was more or less annihilated.

Possibly the most unpopular insect in Changi Camp was the ant which persistently attacked our food supplies, particularly precious delicacies such as sugar. Tins, closed or strung from the roof, were no obstacles. Water we found was our only defence, and to keep our supplies ant-proof, tins had to be isolated in the centre of saucers or bowls of water.

The methods of these ants were extremely interesting, their lives being run on the lines of a well-disciplined army. This was illustrated to a few of us one day as we were brooding in a derelict house in Changi village, an abandoned native village within the perimeter of Changi Camp. On the floor were a few grains of boiled rice, and as we were chatting together, a solitary ant crept in by the window, made a quick reconnaissance round the rice, and then disappeared, no doubt to report to his Commanding Officer. A few minutes later an orderly column of ants crawled in through the window, presumably the Ants Service Corps. After some rapid organisation the ants gathered up the rice, one grain to about six bearers, and in perfect formation crawled out of the window again with their rations.

Rats were not a problem in Changi - there was little enough to eat for the POWs - but they were encountered in large numbers in the camps along the railway and in the ships taking prisoners to Japan. They became such a pest at Tarsau camp after a rice store had been knocked down that the Japs offered a cigarette for every dead rat produced. A total of 125 were produced within the hour. The method was to pour a little petrol down their holes then set fire to it. You would hear an underground explosion, then flaming rats would rush out from a dozen holes, to be beaten to death with great gusto with sticks or boots as they fled.

Jinsen Camp too had its fair share, and at nights we used to hear and feel them as they pattered over our recumbent bodies. Occasionally during the winter months a prisoner would waken up to find a rat sharing his blankets with him for the sake of warmth. We found it difficult to get rid of the rats despite the invention of a rat trap. This was an ingenious Heath Robinson contrivance consisting of a wooden box with a sliding door supported by a few delicately balanced wires. The rat was enticed into the box by a small piece of bait attached to a wire, and when this was touched the door fell, catching the rat alive.

The disposal of the live rat was our principal problem. Although a crowd of bloodthirsty prisoners stood guard, armed with old boots, sticks, and other weapons, quite often the rat escaped when the door was lifted. This difficulty was eventually solved by introducing cats. Our cats arrived more by accident than design. One day a prisoner brought back a stray cat from a working party. Within a few months the cat population had increased to five. The father of the kittens we never knew, but he must have been a bold, buccaneering type. Sentries and barbed wire were certainly no barrier to him in his nocturnal love life.

These cats were all excellent ratters, and on the odd occasion when a rat was caught in our trap, the victim never again escaped. There were always two or three cats on duty waiting to pounce when the door was lifted. The occasional cat found its way into the cooking pot.

As each prison camp was supposed to be self-sufficient as far as possible, the Japs provided us with pigs and rabbits to look after. As far as our rations were concerned, these animals made little difference. On the one occasion when a pig was killed - Christmas 1944 - the Japs generously gave 150 prisoners twenty-five per cent of the pork and kept seventy-five per cent for the Jap staff of about twenty. We did a little better out of the rabbits. Starting off with half a dozen white rabbits, we soon had over a hundred on our hands. About once a week the Japs permitted us to have rabbit soup. The official quota was four rabbits per week for the entire camp. The rabbit register of births and deaths, however, got rather out of hand and generally we were able to slip three or four extra into the pot unbeknown to the Japs.

Another unusual diet was the occasional snake and iguana, a lizard about two feet long. To catch an iguana, a trap was built over a burrow consisting of a bamboo bow, which, when a trigger was released by the lizard sticking its head up, would spring up to tighten a noose around its neck.

Sometimes we would be taken pig hunting in the surrounding jungle. The drill was to form a large circle around a dense patch and work inwards, beating with sticks. There was a fairly large population of feral pigs which had escaped from native villages and if we were lucky as we sometimes were, we would raise one which would make a bolt for freedom. You had to be pretty quick to knock it out as it dashed past, then we would carry it back to camp to put it in a pen when it recovered. However, if there was a Jap anywhere near, the pig would get beaten to a pulp.

Our farm stock certainly provided a hobby for those prisoners who undertook to look after them. For a short time I was the camp's swineherd (or officer in charge of pigs), the stock consisting of four black, hairy pigs of various sizes ranging from a fairly solid sow to a diminutive runt. The conditions under which they existed were primitive. The sty was built by ourselves from stones, logs and mud, and the pigs' rations were even worse than our own. They must have been hardy brutes for they managed to survive on the food scraps of the camp, consisting mainly of fish heads and frozen vegetables in very meagre quantities. Possibly the sparseness of their rations accounted for the extraordinary fact that none grew any larger. I ate my portion of pork with melancholy hunger, like a cannibal making a meal of an old friend.

We certainly had a variety of insect and animal life around us as prisoners of war. In Changi, one or two prisoners even went the length of keeping monkeys as pets. Most of us, however, felt that there were enough *monkeys* around us already. For three and a half years they kept us as their 'pets.'

SNAPSHOT

Some Scots troops often left work on the railway and disappeared into the jungle ostensibly to have a *benjo* but really to have a smoke. One day, the guard, suspicious, caught three of them emerging from the jungle. 'OK, *benjo* me see,' he demanded and marched them back into the jungle. Of course there was nothing to be found and the Jap was just loosening his wrist when they found a mountain of *benjo* left by one of the working elephants. The Jap stared incredulously. 'Very big, *jenika*?' 'No, no. Three men *benjo*,' they replied. The Jap scratched his head, then gave in. 'OK, all men work.'

PEGGY

Colour Sergeant Norman Catto BEM, 2nd Battalion, Gordon Highlanders

No one owned Peggy, but she was the mascot of the 2nd Battalion of The Gordon Highlanders. Peggy was a white bull terrier and was born in Pengerang, our battle station. When we were ordered up country to face the Japs, Peggy came with us in one of our carriers. When we were pushed back, and surrendered in Singapore, Peggy also became a POW. She was in our company the whole of our POW days.

After about three weeks in charge, Major (later Lieutenant Colonel) Reggie Lees who was Battalion Second in Command, and a party of 250 other ranks were marched to Adam Park to build a road round the golf course. Peggy came with us. By this time she was eating rice like us all, although if there were any tit-bits going Peggy always got a fair share.

After about six months we were ordered up to Siam. This journey took five nights and four days: forty men to a steel truck which was very hot during the day but cold at night. Peggy was in our truck. Although there was no room to lie down, she was always given the best place. We eventually arrived in Bampong where we built the bridge across the River Kwai. After some time in this camp Peggy gave birth to two pups underneath our bamboo beds, but five days later the pups disappeared: we think they were killed and eaten.

It was in this camp that any Gordon (Peggy would not go with any other Regiment) wishing to break out of camp to contact the natives always took Peggy for she could smell a Jap long before we could. You had only to say, 'Nips, Peggy,' and she was off like a shot. She received two or three stab wounds for the Japs did not like her.

After about a year we were moved to Kinsayok about sixty miles further up the jungle. Here we spent about another nine months and when that stretch of the line was completed, we went about another sixty miles up country to Konkuita where the line met up with that coming down from Burma. Peggy was with us all the time, staying mostly in the Cookhouse but coming with us to the work site every morning.

We went back to Kanburi in open rail trucks where we spent about four weeks recuperating. We were then sent on to Ubon to build an airfield. After about three months Peggy gave birth to five puppies. When the Japs surrendered about eight weeks later we were taken to Bangkok by train to fly to Rangoon. At first the RAF refused to take the dogs aboard but Colonel Lees persuaded them to look after the pups and Peggy came with us. We stayed in Rangoon for about three weeks, then went to the docks to board a ship. The Captain refused to take Peggy but again Colonel Lees persuaded him to allow her on board. Colour Sergeant James King was in charge of her.

When we arrived in Liverpool, Peggy was taken into quarantine and later rejoined the battalion at Bridge of Don Barracks where I went to see her two or three times. She died on 9th July 1947. Lieutenant Colonel Lees erected a stone of Kemnay granite in her memory on the place where she was buried. When the Bridge of Don Barracks ceased to be a Regimental Depot, Peggy's stone was removed and taken to a site at The Gordon Highlanders' Headquarters at Viewfield Road.

Peggy was granted four medals: 1939/45 Star, Pacific Star, Defence Medal, and War Medal. These are now, together with her photograph, in the Army Museum in London.

Peggy

LUDWIG THE SAUSAGE DOG
J E Whittaker, British Battalion

The dog was a good example of his breed. A sharp intelligent face, nicely rounded head, with a soft velvety ear folded down each side. A smooth brown body that looked impossibly long, ended in an erect whippy tail. His stubby little legs were hardly long enough for his breastbone to clear the ground. He stood at the heel of a man who wore a crumpled and patched pair of shorts, probably once part of his number one khaki drill uniform. A stained officer's cap and a scuffed pair of brown boots were his only other clothes.

The man and dog stood in a group dressed in similar fashion, watching a file of sweat-drenched men enter their camp. On the barely intelligible howl of a Japanese soldier, the leaders halted in front of a line of bamboo huts. With relief they allowed their bundles of possessions to fall from their shoulders, then collapsed alongside them. Their companions, in varying degrees of exhaustion, some assisted by the stronger among them, struggled to join them. The watchers moved towards the new arrivals, but stopped when the Japanese made threatening gestures with their rifles. They sought familiar faces to ask about members of their regiments left in Singapore. But the Nips wanted no mingling whilst counting their charges, prior to handing them over to the camp guards.

It was October 1942, eight months after the disaster of Singapore. In those months captured Australian and British forces had been contained in the extensive barracks area of Changi. Others had been drafted into town to clear war damage and assemble the spoils of victory for shipment to Japan. That comparative period of comfort preceded experiences from which many did not survive. The Japanese began the construction of a railway from Thailand to Burma to supply their armies in their attempt to conquer India. Parties of 600, led by their Officers and NCOs were sent north at regular intervals. To make up numbers, soldiers were detached from their regiments and seconded to other units. The owner of the dachshund was attached to a unit formed from two Infantry battalions which were now in Chungkai, the base of No 2 Railway Construction Group of the Japanese Army. This was sited on the banks of the River Kwai, a few kilometres from the bridge which one day would be famous.

The journey to Chungkai began by train: thirty men plus their possessions to an enclosed metal goods van. On one side only was a door permitted to be open. Stops for relief and food were few as we travelled, in oven heat temperatures, the length of the Malay Peninsula and the Kra

Isthmus. At the rail link with the Thai National Railway, we stopped for two nights, sleeping on boards in huts flooded by monsoon rains, inches above ankle-deep water in which floated the contents washed out of open latrines. The rest of the journey, by lorry, riverboat, and on foot led us eventually to Chungkai.

Chungkai Camp: New Operating Theatre, 1944
Surgeon Sir Edward 'Weary' Dunlop RAAMC conducting an appendix operation under a bamboo frame which held a room-sized mosquito net and where most equipment was make-shift. - G S Gimson

Despite the fatigue it was the surprise of seeing the little dog that occupied some of our conversation between counts and recounts. It was Ludwig, for that was his name, whom we meet again, months after our slog from camp to camp along the line of the river through increasingly difficult terrain and conditions to Burma.

Ludwig's owner in peacetime had served in the Federated Malay States Volunteer Force, a part-time unit recruited from civilian residents: a pleasant enough duty, spending a little spare time training to be a soldier should an emergency arise. But that was hardly conceivable in the days when the British Empire looked unchallengeable. But challenged it was, and in

December 1941, within a few weeks, Malaya was overrun. Ludwig, whilst his master went to war, stayed at home with his mistress, a nurse, but the time came for women and children to be evacuated. She left the doomed island on one of the last escape ships, leaving the dog behind with her husband. By the great good fortune that protects some in wartime, master and dog survived the final Japanese onslaught, then marched into captivity in Changi, sharing meagre rations and scrounging scraps until the move to Thailand.

From Chungkai our unit was sent up river to build bridges and culverts along the narrow track cleared through the jungle by earlier parties. Ill-fed, ill-housed, we worked for the next twelve months without a break through torrential monsoon rains, living in disease-ridden camps until, in October 1943, the line joined the Burmese section on the border at Three Pagodas Pass. With some pomp the Jap High Command came to witness the hammering home of the last spike. The loss of life had been enormous.

Survivors then returned to Chungkai, where, once again we met Ludwig who also had endured the last twelve months elsewhere on the line. The effort to care for the little dog must have added responsibilities which involved some sacrifice.

A large area was now made into a hospital, where medical officers struggled to save life with minimal, often improvised equipment and few medicines. Some entertainment and sports were organised. So too were a number of moneymaking enterprises. Escape projects, as attempted by POWs in Europe, were impossible. Deaths continued as a daily occurrence as the effects of our privations took their toll. Burial parties marched, always with dignity, through the camp to the ever-increasing area of a carefully tended cemetery. For months, a day did not pass without the ceremonial sounding of The Last Post and Reveille. During the silence which overcame the camp, many must have prayed for survival.

But for Ludwig life was not all bad. He enjoyed a pleasure his human companions were denied. He found a girl friend, though not one normally chosen for a chap with such an aristocratic pedigree. She was a skinny mongrel pi-dog who had strayed into the camp from the local *kampongs*. The union resulted in a litter with unmistakable characteristics. Their paternity was beyond doubt, and Ludwig attracted some ribaldry as he walked around camp.

Dachshunds, some say, are one-man dogs. This was true of Ludwig. He spurned efforts by other prisoners to make friends. The periods when he was left alone were spent on his master's bed, and with one exception, anyone who approached met a show of teeth. When his master became so ill that he had to be transferred to the hospital, an officer in the same hut took on the responsibility to feed him. Ludwig accepted his kindness, and never forgot him, permitting a familiarity not shown to others.

The number of pi-dogs in the camp increased, incurring the wrath of the Japanese Camp Commandant. He ordered that all dogs must be removed or shot. To general disbelief this included Ludwig. Protests were unsuccessful. Then a reprieve became possible, but required a decision few would have wished to face. By 1944 Allied bombers were damaging the railway. Rebuilding work was carried out by POWs sent again to remote areas up river. Ludwig's owner, though not high on the list of those judged to be the fittest, volunteered, and the party left with the dog.

Some months later we left the area of the Kwai in a relocation of POW camps - the journey, a torment lasting many days when in turns we carried the older and weaker men on improvised stretchers. With some feelings of despair we wondered how long this could go on.

Then the atom bombs fell. Overnight, without prior rumour, we were free. Repatriation was rapid. Lorries took us to Bangkok from where RAF Dakotas flew us to Rangoon. Telegrams were sent home; we had medical checks, new uniforms, and bought NAAFI luxuries, which, only days before, were the stuff of dreams. In the transit camp were gathered men from other Thailand camps, making it a place of reunions, and exchange of news: some of it sad as hoped-for meetings never took place. One reunion which gave pleasure: Ludwig and his owner were present, safe after their hazardous trip up river.

Checking where we stood in the order of departure, as ships came and went, was a daily activity. If asked though, most would have conceded priority to ex-Malayan residents who had last seen their families in the final days of Singapore. It was known that some of the escape ships had run the gauntlet of enemy attacks. POWs from the East Indies had spoken of sinkings and survivors in women's camps. Ludwig and master were placed on an early draft.

Remembering what happened as they boarded the trooper moored in the Irrawaddy still generates sadness. When they climbed on to the deck they were met with the order 'No dogs allowed.' In that moment, after three and a half years of sacrifice, hardship and reciprocated devotion, a choice had to be made: travel to Singapore, the best source of news of his wife, or stay with the little dog and chance that another ship would take them. Not unnaturally, the choice made was to go to Singapore, while Ludwig returned to shore. A sympathetic nurse in the Army hospital volunteered to care for him, but one wonders what emotions the little fellow experienced by this sudden separation from his close companion of so many years.

Some months after our return to the UK a tribute was published in the *In Memoriam* column of the Daily Telegraph. The essence of the tribute was, 'In tender, loving and sweet memory, on this her birthday ... formerly Federated Malay States, evacuated from Singapore Feb 13 1942. She survived the sinking of the *Kuala*, the horrors of Pom Pom Island and the sinking of the *Tanjong Pinang*, but was missing from a raft in the Java seas. *'All she had she gave for others.'*

No one I have met knows whether the man and dog were reunited. One question, on a lighter note, recurs. Are there, in the *kampongs* where our camp was sited, any of Ludwig's descendants? And, if there are any genetic throwbacks, with unusually long bodies or short legs, do the locals ever wonder why?

SNAPSHOT
In hospital in Rangoon at the end, Matron sailed into the ward, all starch and elbows: an awe-inspiring sight and unlike anything Ludwig, lying under his master's bed, had ever set eyes on. So he yapped. At the sound Matron turned and said, 'Put that dog out.' His master protested, 'But Ma'am he's been with us through it all.' But she, quite reasonably replied, 'A hospital is no place for a dog,' and turned to leave. She was stopped by a strange rustling noise and turned to find all the men in the ward rolling up their bedding. 'If Ludwig goes, we all go.' She hesitated, and then, to her eternal credit, said, 'Very well then, he can stay.' - G S Gimson

PART VII
The Closing Days

Dysentery Ward, Kanyu Camp

*The layout of the dysentery ward was the same as the living-huts, giving no easy access for the orderlies who included both medical corps personnel and volunteer troops. At the time of this sketch, the one and only Medical Officer had no medicines except a small supply of Epsom Salts which was not suitable for the predominant amoebic dysentery. The sketch shows the state of the ward **before** the monsoon rains reduced everything to muddy squalor and the 'speedo' (the vicious drive to push on the building of the railway) reduced the men to an even worse state than before. Conditions then were indescribable. - G S Gimson*

THE LAST MOVE
Charles Hugh, Edinburgh

We lived on rumours! Good rumours, bad rumours, or merely silly rumours; they were all grist to our mill. But nobody took much notice of a rumour of another move. At the officers' camp at Kanburi we had had rumours of a move for months. Now it was a reality. The advance party had gone, so had parties numbers one and two. All we, of No 3 party, knew was that the new camp was being built in hill country at a place called Nakom Nyok, about eighty miles north-east of Bangkok.

Our camp commandant, Captain Noguchi, had told us with relish that we had some heavy marching to do, some thirty or forty miles to be done in one day. It was the usual arrangement about kit. As you could take what you could carry on your back, heavy marching meant lightening your kit by throwing away all the little things that had helped to make life in camp a bit more comfortable. Thirty miles is nothing to a fit man in decent conditions, but we had to do it after being cooped up, 3,500 of us, in a camp about three hundred yards long by two hundred yards broad and we did not care for the prospect.

There was something else which made the journey especially unwelcome. The Americans and the RAF were making a proper job of smashing up the Railway. Nobody relished the idea of being crammed thirty-two to a truck in a troop train while the boys in the Liberators were doing their stuff. Sergeant Shimozo, to our regret, was to be in charge of the party. Shimozo was a really bad Nip, an able assistant to Noguchi and nearly as wicked. He had the most unpleasant face I have ever seen and I have seen quite a few. He was in the advanced stages of an unspeakable disease and was booked for a painful death.

The day before we moved, Noguchi made a speech about discipline during the journey. We were to remember that we were British officers and not beggars and therefore we were not to stoop to accepting any gifts that the Thais might try to pass to us during the journey. Said to a crowd of haggard men dressed in rags or three parts naked, burned black with the sun and all stinking like polecats, this remark was very droll. It was particularly appreciated by those of us who had worked as coolies on the Siam-Burma railway.

The following evening we paraded to march out. When a mountain of camp stores had been loaded on the train we sat in the trucks for hours waiting for the train to start. At last Shimozo, all sword and teeth, ordered the guards on to the train and got on himself. The train started amid cheers, crawled for about four hundred yards and stopped again. We had another long wait and ate some of the rations we carried with us - boiled rice, peanuts and pumpkin - while the sun went down. Finally we started in earnest and as the cool breeze played around us our spirits rose. As darkness fell, tension relaxed - the railway was usually spared in the hours before sunset.

At length we reached Nom Pladuk. This was a big prison camp which had been rather badly hit in one or two of the air raids on the big marshalling yards at this place. Suddenly a hush fell on the trucks and men sat up, listening intently. There was no mistaking the drone of approaching aircraft. A moment later pandemonium broke loose, the Japanese shouting and yelling at us while we climbed out of the trucks and were doubled away in parties to the cover of some trees a little way beyond the railroad. Meanwhile some of us were put to off-loading grenades and ammunition from our train and dumping the boxes in a place of safety. The aircraft, a single bomber, made a circuit of the area and moved off, only to return and finally leave for good.

My memory of the next day is mainly of heat, intense thirst, and cramp. In the afternoon we halted at a small station where more trucks were added to our train. They were steel goods-trucks and were packed with Japanese sick and wounded from Burma. Although we did not think that anything would make us feel sorry for the Japanese, the condition of these Japanese casualties appalled us. They were crowded into the trucks, where the heat as we had cause to know, was dreadful. Advanced malaria, battle casualties with their first field dressings still unchanged, officers and men alike, they lay in their own filth with no bedding, no water, no cigarettes and no attention. After all, the poor devils were fighting soldiers, wounded and sick through fighting for their Emperor, yet the back-line scum in charge of us not only would do nothing for them, but shouted and kicked them out of the way. It was left for us to do what we could. We had not been ordered to assist by our guards. This was *bushido*.

That evening we reached a big river, the bridge over which had been smashed by the Allied air force. Repairs had been done and it was possible to manhandle one or two trucks over what was left of the bridge and this some of us had to do. The remainder had to shift stores and kit to the far side of the river, a distance of about a mile, where another train had to be loaded. Water was drawn from the river and put on to boil while thirsty men hung round the fires hardly able to wait till it was made ready to drink. Meanwhile, a party of fifty officers was detailed to go and fill up the boiler of a railway engine with water. This was done by drawing water in buckets from a nearby paddy-field, the full buckets being passed by a chain up to the engine.

By now darkness had fallen. When eventually we were ready to entrain we found that the rolling stock provided was not very much more than half that which we had travelled in before and the trucks this time were of the closed pattern. As far as loading men on to trains is concerned the Japanese are able to put a quart into a pint pot but getting the whole party on to that train was almost too much even for them. Eventually we were all on the train, clinging to the roof and hanging on wherever there was a foothold.

In the middle of the night the train reached Bangkok station and then began a period which is still in our minds as a bedlam of order and counter order, shouts and yells, curses and blows. Shimozo had of course lost his temper in the proceedings and had gone into the uncontrollable rage which seems to be usual among the Japanese when they are faced with any difficulty. His soldiers who were terrified of him lost their heads and made us their whipping boys, though in fairness it must be said that some of them continued to behave with moderation.

Dawn found us approaching a cluster of wharf and store godowns some miles down the river from Bangkok City. Here we were to have two days rest in preparation for the train journey and the march to follow. We soon discovered that the local Japanese commandant was a disciplinarian, which in the Japanese army means a bully. Whenever he entered the godown, we had to get up and stand to attention and he made a point of coming in very frequently.

The long-expected incident occurred the following day. The Thais had been very friendly and had been making efforts to pass us cigarettes and messages of goodwill. Unfortunately, when two officers were on their way to the latrines, a Thai lorry driver threw them a packet of cigarettes which they attempted to pick up. They were seen by a guard and arrested. There was a tremendous 'to do' and the Japanese commandant was very soon solemnly trying the case. The trial was doubtless fair but the two officers concerned had no opportunity of forming an opinion on the point for they had to stand outside the office while the case was being heard. Later they were taken away by the Japanese Military Police and very severely beaten.

On the next day we moved in very slow stages down to Bangkok Station. We were much cheered to see the heavy damage done by our air force to the various installations we passed on the way, and our Korean guards who were seeing heavy bomb damage for the first time, seemed much impressed. When we got to the station we found that it had suffered tremendously in recent air raids. At long last we left the station and the train continued on its way past interminable paddy-fields.

At some point in the small hours, while it was still pitch dark, we arrived at the little station where we were to detrain for the march. But none of us had worn boots regularly for a considerable time and soft feet demanded steady going, especially when heavy loads have to be carried. Shimozo cared for none of these things and mounting his pony, he set off at a pace so fast that those of us at the rear of the column nearly had to double if we would escape the attention of the guards behind us. We completed the first seventeen and a half kilometres before the sun was well up. There were no proper halts, only a few short pauses while one or two elderly Dutchmen who had fallen by the wayside were encouraged to resume the march. The fast pace soon told on our feet and many of us acquired blisters.

Soon after sunrise we had our first proper halt. We were met by lorries from the camp bringing us a meal. After twenty minutes we resumed the march. The sun climbed into the sky with tropical intensity and it was already too hot for comfort. For all of us this march will bring a picture of unending red laterite road bordered with a few scattered trees stretching away until it was lost in the interminable distance. On either side of us were paddy fields unfolding in green monotony. Occasionally we saw a small village in the distance; now and then we passed through one.

Not many of us can remember much detail of the halts which we were permitted to make. None of them can have lasted longer than a quarter of an hour and they consisted of a scramble for water no matter where it came from - paddy-fields, buffalo wallows that contained water - and the colour did not matter. We broke every law of hygiene every day of the last three years anyway.

For the first few steps after each halt the pain in our feet was acute. The men staggered rather than walked. Then one's feet regained their normal level of discomfort and one took up a steady rhythm once again. One trouble was that the halts never came at regular intervals but at the whim of Shimozo who sometimes rode and sometimes walked.

In the early afternoon when we were really beginning to feel the strain, we did a stretch of over ten kilometres at an increased pace. By then the heat was intense and this part of the march was a Waterloo for many. Eventually we reached a crossroads and turned off the road we had been following so long. Packs seemed lighter and we quickened our pace. We reached the camp and halted outside while Shimozo went in. Tea was brought out to us. Our spirits soared.

Then a disquieting rumour grew to fact. This was not our camp: our camp lay between five and seven kilometres further on. We fell in and moved on again while the shadows rapidly lengthened into dusk. About 700 yards further on, when our feet were just getting nicely numb again, we met a lorry, sent out from our own camp, with tea and rice and vegetable stew. We halted once more, and those who could had a meal. Shimozo had now become strangely solicitous of our welfare.

We turned off the main road and entered on a newly made track with a surface that left much to be desired. We kept our eyes on the back of the man in front, not knowing and hardly caring whether our next footstep would fall on level ground or into a hole. Now and then there was a crash and a curse as somebody fell, his kit scattering in the darkness. We began to get strange hallucinations now. Men frequently saw the huts and fence of a big camp where there was no camp. Others saw light, some saw towers and minarets.

At long last we really did see lights. We had arrived. Now followed an endless wait while the Japanese tried to count us. While we waited, a heavy tropical thunderstorm broke over the camp and in a moment we were soaked to the skin and our kit and blankets saturated. Finally the Japanese gave up trying to count us and we moved off following guides with lanterns who were to lead us to our huts through the pitch dark camp. Long bamboo huts with cut grass spread on the earth floor. Cooks brought food for us. A steaming mud-smeared mob, jostling while each man tried to find somewhere to drop his pack. Cigarettes and a buzz of conversation. We looked round for a dry bit of ground, unrolled our sodden blankets and lay down. We did not know it, but we had completed our last journey as prisoners of war.

Originally published in Blackwoods Magazine April 1946.

SNAPSHOT

Apart from bombing the railway the Allied planes sometimes dropped morale-boosting leaflets telling us about their successes in Burma and the Pacific. One leaflet ended with the words 'It's in the bag'. The ensuing search by the Japs for the bag went on for days. The Jap interpreter called in all reading matter held by the POWs for censorship. All bibles and prayer books were returned, including a copy of *The Saint in New York*. But bible maps such as 'Jerusalem in the time of Herod' had been torn out!

JOURNEY'S END

G S Gimson

There were few of us who doubted that the Allies would, in the end, defeat Japan. What we did doubt was whether we would be alive to see that day. Again, few failed to realise that the final stages would almost certainly be catastrophic for us. Whether we were still in areas which became battle-grounds, or were force-marched away from these areas, or simply eliminated as an encumbrance to the Japs, the end promised disaster. I wonder if anyone foresaw that there might be a 'clean break' such as was brought about by the atom bomb. In early 1945, the digging of deep moats round the camps stimulated the dread of what was about to happen, and, aided by hints from Koreans, pointed to the possibility of massacre. It was remarkable that the dig itself, by naked POWs toiling in water often polluted by latrine seepage, did not do the job for the Japs. From then on, as the signs of Allied domination increased, it became abundantly clear that the 'final solution' would not be long delayed.

Here is how the final stages developed in one camp: the officers' camp at Nakom Nayok. Officers had been segregated, with only a few ORs - camp 'tradesmen' such as cooks - at Kanburi in about January 1945. There were about 3,000 officers in all. From late in June 1945, parties of 200 were despatched by train to a new camp at Nakom Nayok, east of Bangkok. They were told not to accept fruit or tobacco from natives: 'Remember you are officers, not beggars', although at that stage, it would have been difficult to tell the difference!

Final (Officers') Camp, Nakom Nayok. Allies' Flags Faintly Visible

At least two of the parties were involved in remarkable incidents when their trains were standing in a marshalling yard at Non Pladuk. Japanese hospital trains from the Burmese front pulled into nearby sidings. They consisted of open trucks and carried both sick and wounded Japs. It was quite clear that they had had no medical attention although they must have been at least three days from any battle area. The wounded still had only their 'first field dressings'. Moreover, on the occasion which I witnessed, a Japanese medical officer in a spotless white coat walked about without approaching the patients or showing any interest. Sentries drove some of the patients who could walk to fetch food from a ration point, hitting them and shouting. Our own ORs (the train carried a party from one of the men's camps) watched this, and began to growl menacingly. They then took what fruit and tobacco they could get over to the Jap patients. When you think that thousands of our mates had already died through Japanese cruelty, this was an astonishing demonstration of human feeling.

The journey took five days in all, ending with a thirty-one mile march, carrying all our kit. The new camp-site was about 400 yards square, completely flat and providing no cover from air or ground attack. Huts were under construction. The site was at a fairly high altitude and the air pleasantly fresh. The work of construction was heavy, but was for our own benefit. The Jap Commandant was Captain Noguchi from Kanburi, a sadistic but intelligent (and therefore dangerous) man. He had set up a small factory in the camp at Kanburi for the production of soap and dyes, presumably for his own profit, using any POWs with experience in chemistry. The Senior POW officer was Colonel Toosey, one of the true heroes of the captivity.

Nothing in particular occurred to heighten the tension until, in August, and unknown to all but Colonel Toosey and his 'staff', a Korean (named Haria I believe) asked the British interpreter, Greig, to take him to speak to Toosey. It transpired that Haria, who was intelligent and literate, had seen an order on Noguchi's desk instructing him that on the anticipated Allied attack on the Japs in Thailand, all POWs *and all Korean sentries* were to be killed. The Japs obviously did not consider the Koreans reliable.

Toosey arranged that on the order being given for the massacre, Haria should bring all the Koreans, who were by far the majority of guards in the camp, with all the weapons in the guard-hut (probably only about twelve rifles and one or two light automatics) to a rendezvous. There, selected POW marksmen would take over the weapons and do what they could to hold off the attack while the rest tried to disperse into the nearby jungle. Each of us was ordered to prepare a sharpened bamboo spear to be hidden in the thatch above our bed space. At some stage, it became known that two Japanese machine-gun companies were stationed near the camp to carry out the massacre. The weapons in the camp would have been of little use against them.

Apart from the obvious inference from the order to prepare spears - that Toosey feared some form of trouble - nothing further was known by the generality of POWs.

The secret wireless-set from Kanburi had been transferred to the new camp, passed off as part of the equipment of Noguchi's factory, but there were no batteries and it could not be used. Eventually, on the night of 16th August, the operators 'borrowed' the battery from Noguchi's car at about midnight, and tuned in to All-India Radio. The first thing they heard was part of the News: 'General MacArthur has flown to Tokyo to take control.' From this, it was obvious that Japan had surrendered. Toosey was told immediately, and ordered that no one else, other than anyone whom he considered must know, should be told lest there be any form of demonstration. It was not known whether Noguchi knew of the surrender, and he was plainly capable of treating any demonstration as a mutiny or even merely as an excuse to anticipate the order for massacre. It must have been a moment of quite overwhelming emotion, yet the operators of the radio and Toosey himself managed to conceal their excitement. It was about twenty-four hours later when Noguchi, who had returned from a summons to Bangkok, made a few untypical relaxations of rules without explanation, that Toosey went to him and asked what had happened. Noguchi replied that the war had ended - but did not say how, or who had won.

Even then, knowing that Jap troops in the vicinity would not necessarily believe or obey orders so unthinkable to them, Toosey ordered that there should only be the most low-key of reactions. In the evening, the POWs gathered on a slope in the camp, and quietly sang their national anthems (British, Dutch and American) and the doxology and all then dispersed. The Allied flags were hoisted. A Jap with a sewing machine was made to prepare an American flag with its many stars and stripes, and there was also a tiny French flag for the one Frenchman in the camp.

A couple of days later, an American commando who had been 'underground' in the jungle for some months, came to the camp and told us some of the world news, but would say nothing about his mission, apparently lest the Jap troops fought on. There followed a couple of excited but wearisome weeks before evacuation to Bangkok and flight to Rangoon. At Bangkok airport civilian internees set up a tea-urn with a capacity of perhaps thirty cups for about 3000 POWs. Few took any notice until the Swedish consul's blonde daughter appeared at the urn, when the queue numbered about 2,999!

View from Tail-board of Lorry Leaving Nakom Nayok Camp on the Journey to the Free World

Released ex-prisoners are taken to Bangkok Airport to be flown to Rangoon as the first stage of their repatriation - a moment of overwhelming excitement for which only ten minutes sketching-time was available! - G S Gimson

In Rangoon, since no preparations had been possible for the sudden unexpected arrival of some 25,000 ex-POWs, there were neither food stocks nor cooking facilities for us. All service units were therefore put on half rations, and they cooked for, and fed, an equivalent number of ex-POWs with the other half. Naturally, there was great discussion of our various experiences. A group from my regiment, being guests at a RAF mess, learned that the RAF had planned to attack our camp at Nakom Nayok on 18th August, with fifteen Liberator bombers and eighteen Mosquito fighter-bombers. It was thought to be a Jap army transit camp since it was in the middle of their third line of defence, and in accordance with Jap practice, was not marked with the Red Cross. If that had taken place - and we missed it by only three days - there would have been few survivors left to be dealt with by the Japs.

On a lighter note. One party from Kanburi was on transit at Bangkok when news of the Jap surrender reached the Japs and Thais. The Thai engine driver tried to walk along to the POW trucks to tell them, but the Japs prevented him. He went back to his engine, uncoupled it, put up a board chalked 'UK US V' and drove his engine along an adjoining siding past the POW trucks, to be greeted with ecstatic cheering.

For my own part, it was only when we were safely landed in Rangoon that the threat of disaster really evaporated, and the whole of the nightmare experience receded into history. Our captivity had lasted precisely three and a half years to the day: 15th February 1942 to 15th August 1945.

Nakom Nayok Camp after the Japanese Surrender
POW officers are depicted here in their bed spaces on the ground. - G S Gimson

THE FINAL SOLUTION

Excerpt from the Tokyo War Crimes Trials Document No 2701 Certified as Exhibit 'O' in Document 2687 from the Journal of the Taiwan POW Camp HQ in Taihoku

Instructions were issued to Camp Commandants that in the event of Allied invasion of Japanese-occupied territory, all prisoners of war were to be exterminated in whatever way was most convenient in local circumstances.

'At such time as the situation became urgent and it be extremely important, the POWs will be concentrated and confined in their present location and under heavy guard the preparation for the final disposition will be made. The time and method of this disposition are as follows:

(1) The Time. Although the basic aim is to act under superior orders, individual disposition may be made;

(2) The Method. (a) Whether they are destroyed individually or in groups, or however it is done, with mass bombing, poisonous smoke, poisons, drowning, decapitation, or what, dispose of them as the situation dictates. (b) In any case it is the aim not to allow the escape of a single one, to annihilate them all, and not to leave any traces.

I hereby certify that this is a true translation from the Journal of the Taiwan POW HQ in Taiwan entry 1 August 1944. Signed Stephen H Green. Sworn before me this 19th day of September 1946.

Excerpt from
OPERATION RANGOON JAIL
Col K P MacKenzie, RAMC

We stopped every hour and at the end of each resting period there were always two men beside me to drag me along and to speak a few words of comfort and good cheer. For the last two hours the burden was borne by Sergeants Handsell and Martin. They did more for me, as did the others, than any man had any reasonable right to expect. They had had no food themselves for forty-eight hours and they were in a distressed condition. Most of the time I was in a state of coma. In a lucid moment I asked Handsell if I had talked a lot. He confirmed that I was in a state of delirium most of the time.

These two stalwarts were with me when we halted about seven o'clock on the morning of 29th April at a small village on the Pegu-Wau road. Here I asked O'Hari San if I could have an interview with the Jap Commandant for I had come to my decision. O'Hari asked me why I wanted to see the commandant. I replied that it was a personal matter, but when he announced that he was not prepared to forward my request unless I gave a reason, I was too weary to argue any further. I drew upon my reserves and said, 'Please, O'Hari San, get the Commandant. I am finished. I cannot march any further. My legs and feet are useless and I am impeding the progress of my friends. I have disposed of my kit and, before we leave here tonight I want the Commandant to do me a personal favour. I want him to put a bullet through my heart. I will mark the place on my shirt with a piece of paper or mark my chest with a coloured pencil. The sooner the better, Mr O'Hari, please, so that I may be buried before the column moves off again.' O'Hari appeared stunned and called around him a group of Japanese NCOs. They jabbered away amongst themselves excitedly but nobody made any move to fetch the Commandant.

The next thing I knew was that Brigadier Hobson was called up to speak with the Commandant. When he went, I lay under a *banyan* tree, not caring much what happened now. Within half an hour Brigadier Hobson called out to our bewildered assembly of nearly 400 prisoners, 'We are free, we are free!'

I lay there unable to take in the news and was almost instantaneously surrounded by thirty or forty NCOs and men shouting, 'You've made it', Congratulations Sir,' or 'Well done, Colonel, well done'. I could not speak but I held my hand out feebly and one by one my companions ran up and shook it. It was perhaps the proudest moment of my life. It made me realise that what little I had been able to do for the splendid fellows in the way of doctoring, and by being, as far as I could, their guide, philosopher, and friend, was deeply appreciated.

It soon got round that the Jap Commandant had told Hobson that he had decided that the march must be abandoned and that he and his men must return to Rangoon. They were giving up responsibility for the prisoners and passing over command to Hobson. Within a few minutes the Japs marched quickly away from us in an opposite direction to Rangoon!

Hobson took over a Burmese hut in the village as an office and I was helped over to a small room, above his office. Shouts warned us that there were Allied aircraft overhead. Hobson rushed to my side and pulled and lifted me on to the floor and then lay down beside me. A forty-three pound bomb exploded just outside sending bomb splinters and pieces of the structure flying in all directions. Neither of us was hurt. Then the aircraft began to machine-gun us. The first bullet from them hit Hobson squarely in the right kidney region and inflicted a deep wound. Blood was pouring from the wound and Brigadier Hobson was dead. Poor Hobson! He was destroyed by our own side after the years he had suffered at the hands of the enemy. He died in the moment of his triumph, for surely it was his finest hour, when shortly before, he stood in front of us, waving a piece of paper and announcing to us all, 'We are free.'

If the aircraft had come over a few minutes later, we might well have been spared the final disaster of Hobson's death, for Duckenfield and his men had ready their Union Jack and had also prepared from white pieces of cloth a massive notice: FOUR HUNDRED BRITISH PRISONERS HERE. NO FOOD. SOS. These were now spread on the ground and four men stood near each corner with bits of mirror in their hands. Our message was picked up by a Spitfire pilot who pinpointed our position on his map and informed the nearest Brigade Headquarters.

SAVED FROM FRIENDLY FIRE

Hugh McMichael CA, Vice-Chairman SFEPOW Association

Hugh McMichael was a fighter pilot flying Beaufighters out of southern India. He and his observer were shot down off Akyab in Burma and landed in the water. After being in the sea for five hours he managed to reach the shore to be faced with two Japs with fixed bayonets. He was interned at Rangoon Jail for two and a half years.

Rangoon Jail was the camp used by the Japanese to house Allied POWs captured in Burma. It had been built by the British and was a good solid building divided up into different sections. On 1st May 1945 Rangoon Jail was still the home of some hundreds of prisoners of war. Those who were fit and reasonably able had been marched out of the jail by the Japanese to be used as hostages in the face of the 14th Army approaching the city from the north.

Although the Japanese had fled from Rangoon, Allied aircraft continued to bomb the city, apparently unaware that the Japanese had already gone. Those of us who were left decided to paint messages on the roof of the buildings: 'Japs Gone' and 'British Here' hoping the airmen would get the message. But the air attacks continued as the airmen thought it was a trick.

A fellow RAF pilot and I decided to paint another message on yet another roof: 'Extract Digit'. There was no way the Japs would know that expression. It worked, and no more bombs were dropped near the jail. Three days later we were free. The naval assault vessels had arrived at the mouth of the Rangoon river and were surprised to find that we, the prisoners, were in fact in charge of the jail and the Japs had gone - without a fight.

SNAPSHOT

At Nakom Nayok, there were separate camps for Officer POWs and Other Ranks. After the Japanese surrender and before any Allied personnel had appeared, Lady Mountbatten visited the OR camp. While in Rangoon I heard the following anecdote: When the RSM who was in command of the men's camp learned that Lady M was on her way to visit them, he realised that there might be one problem - there was no ladies' loo. So he mobilised a couple of carpenters and a slab of teak, plus the materials for a bamboo screen, and in next to no time, there was a loo of which Shanks of Barrhead would have been proud. As Lady Mountbatten was leaving, the RSM mentioned that she was leaving some disappointed men behind. She asked, 'How so?' - and he explained. She replied, 'I'm very sorry but in this heat, I can't oblige, but if you like I'll autograph the seat.' And she did. (Imperial War Museum alert?) - Stanley Gimson.

PART VIII
The Japanese Surrender

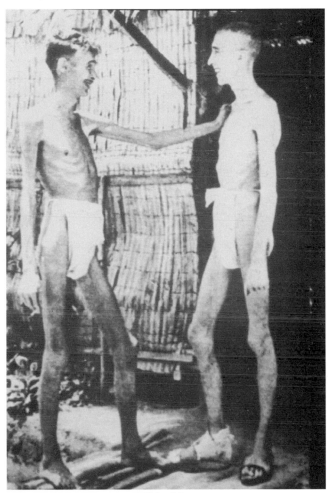

Thin Men

These men would have caused little surprise in many of the camps except for their obvious happiness, but that was due to the news of Japan's surrender. Two Medical Officers from the camps have confirmed that these men would have been considered fit for labour.

THE ATOM BOMBS

America, having established air bases in the Marianas, began systematic high-altitude strikes in daylight on Japan's industrial centres in early 1945. These, however, were less effective than had been anticipated and new tactics were decided upon. Low-level night strikes with napalm firebombs provided instant and unexpected success. During one such attack in March 1945, approximately twenty-five per cent of the flimsy wood and plaster buildings of Tokyo were destroyed and more than 80,000 inhabitants were killed. A further million were rendered homeless.

So successful had been the preliminary raids, and at so little cost in American lives, that it appeared as though Japan might eventually, as a result of such tactics, be bombed into surrender without the necessity of the deadly cost of armed invasion. Other raids on Osaka, Kobe, Yokohama and other major cities therefore followed, all equally devastating.

Yet a far more effective weapon was about to be placed in the hands of Allied tacticians, a weapon so terrifying in its explosive power that it could leave no doubt of a speedy resolution to the conflict.

In 1939, shortly before the outbreak of the European war, Albert Einstein had warned President Roosevelt that Nazi Germany was conducting experiments in the possible use of nuclear fission as the agent of an unprecedentedly explosive power. Should those experiments succeed, he argued, the Nazis would have access to a weapon of such terrible ascendancy, they would be irresistible.

It was not until 1941, however, that America finally undertook what became known as the Manhattan Project with the US Office of Scientific Research and Development and the War Department jointly setting up the intensive research which finally resulted in the atomic bomb. The first experimental device was successfully exploded at Alamogordo on 16ᵗʰ July 1945 with a power equivalent to 15,000 tons of TNT. Less than a month later, a lone plane flew high over Hiroshima to usher in the atomic era.

POWs SAW BOMB DROPPED

Excerpt from 'Incredible Journey' by Barry Reid

On 9th August, Aidan MacCarthy, RAF Squadron Leader and doctor, remembered that the day began bright and clear. High above, he saw eight vapour trails - two four-engine bombers heading south. Then the planes turned back toward Nagasaki. MacCarthy and his men scrambled for their air raid shelter. Several POWs did not bother to go into the pit and kept gazing at the vapour trails. One shouted down to MacCarthy that three small parachutes had been dropped. Then followed a blue atomic flash, accompanied by a bright, magnesium-type flare. Next came a deafening explosion, followed by a blast of hot air that shuddered through ventilation slits in the concrete. An eerie silence followed. After an interminable interval, an Australian stuck his head up, looked around and ducked back in, his face a sheet of white.

The POWs scrambled to the exits, then halted in their tracks. The camp had disappeared, the wooden huts carbonised to ashes. Bodies were everywhere. The brick guardroom had collapsed. They could see clearly up the length of the valley where previously factories and buildings had formed a screen. Left behind was a crazy forest of corrugated sheets clinging to twisted girders. Just outside the prison gate there had been a tall building of the Mitsubishi Company where 500 young women had worked. 'Where the building had been hit,' MacCarthy remembered, 'they had been catapulted out, spread as a human carpet up to a distance of nearly a thousand feet, giving the impression of a nightmare doll factory. The majority lay as if asleep, unmarked and unburnt, still in their trouser suits, and seeming as though they were waiting to be replaced on a massive shelf.' Most frightening was the lack of sunlight. It was a kind of twilight. MacCarthy genuinely thought it was the end of the world.

MacCarthy and the other surviving prisoners turned and made for the foothills north of the valley. *En route* they were sickened by an endless stream of burned, bleeding, flesh-torn, stumbling people, many unable to rise from where they had fallen. The whole atmosphere was permeated by blind terror, and the macabre twilight was illuminated by numerous fires, the crackle of which mixed with the screams of the injured and dying. Thousands of people scrambled, pushed, shoved and crawled across the shattered landscape seeking safety.

Fearing that the Japanese locals would tear them apart, MacCarthy said he was a doctor and at once started administering to the burned and the dying. He splinted broken bones, using native fernlike leaves to ease the pain.

'I seriously wondered,' said MacCarthy, 'whether we had finally arrived at Judgement Day - an angry God was devastating the Japanese for their sins, and mistakenly including us in the holocaust.'

MacCarthy and his group were rounded up by the *Kampeti*, or secret police, and marched back to what was left of the camp. The POWs who had remained on the surface had been incinerated. Others were now blind. For the next five days MacCarthy's group was marched from a new camp down into the centre of the valley where they assisted in cremating victims. Bodies were laid on piles of wood, sprayed with oil, and set afire. On the morning of 15th August, MacCarthy awoke to find the camp deserted. The guards reappeared two hours later, dressed in their best uniforms. The commandant emerged from his office also in full dress. At noon there was a blast of martial music followed by the voice of the emperor. All bowed low as he announced the surrender.

As a major, MacCarthy was the highest-ranking officer among the prisoners, and he called a conference of the senior men of each nationality. They decided to visit the commandant at once. They rang the assembly bell and gathered all of the POWs into the compound. In a voice faltering with emotion, MacCarthy announced the great news. 'We cried, hugged each other, dropped to our knees and thanked God.' MacCarthy accepted the commandant's sword and placed him in a guardroom cell for his own protection. A number of POWs had been all set to hang him immediately.

The prisoners though were still in danger. There were no American troops in Japan, and they were at the mercy of the population. MacCarthy issued daily security bulletins. No one was to leave camp unless in armed groups, and there was to be no drinking of local *saki*. On the second day of freedom, American soldiers parachuted into Nagasaki. They instructed MacCarthy to paint POW signs on the roofs of the buildings. Next, food, medicine and clothing were air dropped. MacCarthy found it hard to believe that the brutality, the beatings and starvings were over and that the recent holocaust was real, not a nightmare. Survival had been against all possible odds.

In retrospect, despite the appalling treatment and his own suffering, MacCarthy felt little bitterness toward the Japanese. Their totally different culture and religion made them so alien that he could not regard their actions as immoral. Everything his own world stood for had been turned on its head during his imprisonment.

The war over, MacCarthy, with a little reluctance, faced life again. 'But I faced life with a very different attitude. For a considerable period I had lived from one day to the next, rejoicing in the fact that I was surviving in the short term. Now I was able to plan in the long term. Even now I thank God for the miracle of being alive. I also thank God for the villagers who prayed for me and produced such a wonderfully strong battery of prayer. But the greatest gift I have had is the appreciation of life around me. To be able to love my wife and children, to breathe the air, to see a tree in the golden stillness of a Cork evening, to take a glass of Irish whiskey, to see my children grow up, to fish in the grey-green waters of my favourite river - and to see the dawn come up on a new day.'

Aidan MacCarthy died at his Northwood home on 11th October 1995 at the age of eighty-three, and is buried in West Cork, Ireland. He was having a brandy and listening to his own voice on a taped BBC broadcast at the time of his death.

PLANE CRASHED CARRYING POWS

Flight 66 of 117 Squadron RAF Dakota left Rangoon Mingladoon on the 8th September 1945 for Saigon to evacuate British Prisoners of War who had been prisoners under the Japanese for three and a half years. All were suffering from starvation and tropical diseases. On arrival, the plane loaded with twenty-four POWs and the RAF crew of four, took off on the return flight, landing at Bangkok to refuel. About 1 pm on that day, villagers of Nuaunggangale, about thirteen miles north west of Moulmein in Burma, and about one hundred and fifty miles south east of the final destination of Rangoon, heard an aircraft out at sea followed by an explosion. The same evening at high tide they found various articles washed ashore and the next day at low tide saw the wreckage scattered over a sandbank. Several unidentified bodies were recovered but no trace of any survivors was found.

HOW THE GOOD NEWS CAME TO SOME
Major Archie Black

Towards the end of July 1945 I was towed up the Mekong River from Saigon on a large-rice barge. It was decked over for most of its length and kept us waterproof. Unfortunately it also kept out fresh air but as we were allowed on top, that was not too much hardship. There were four of these barges, each carrying 250 POWs, and we were told our destination was up near the Siamese Chinese border where we were to build an airfield.

Some years later I read in a book by an American historian that our journey's end was Dien Bien Phu where the French were savaged by the Vietminh nine years later. Desdbed, a malarial ridden pestilential hollow in the hills, would probably have been journey's end for most of us but providence, or the atomic bomb which we did not know about, intervened. You may choose according to your own persuasion but my money is on technology.

We stopped at Phnom Penh for a few days, then returned to Saigon. Something had happened! The normally cowed French - and they had every reason to be - were waving and cheering. Lights were fully on. But our guards remained as taciturn as always. Probably they knew more than we did. After we disembarked we were lined up and counted. As usual, that took several attempts even though we had gone metric and were in files of five. When they were satisfied with the count or had given up, the river guard disappeared and a new guard marched us back to our ex-Foreign Legion barracks on the east side of the river. We noted the weapon slits on strong points had been turfed over. Then we were marched in single file down the side of the barracks' wall to enter singly through a narrow doorway. We did not like that and I listened intently for any untoward noises from the inside, but all was quiet.

As I entered, my hand was gripped by a small Australian with the words, ' The Blue is over.' Well, the war was over but the violence and danger remained. However, as Rudyard Kipling is reported to have said, 'That is another story.'

THE JAPANESE SURRENDER

News of Hiroshima's destruction was only slowly understood in Tokyo. Many members of the Japanese government did not appreciate the power of the new Allied weapon until after the Nagasaki attack. Meanwhile, on 8th August, the USSR had declared war against Japan. The combination of these developments tipped the scales within the government in favour of a group that had, since the spring, been advocating a negotiated peace.

On 10th August the Japanese government issued a statement agreeing to accept the surrender terms of the Potsdam Declaration on the understanding that the emperor's position as a sovereign ruler would not be prejudiced. In their reply the Allies granted Japan's request that the emperor's sovereign status be maintained, subject only to their supreme commander's directives. Japan accepted this proviso on 15th August, and the emperor Hirohito urged his people to accept the decision to surrender.

It was a bitter pill to swallow, though, and every effort was made to persuade the Japanese to accept the defeat that they had come to regard as unthinkable. Even princes of the Japanese Imperial House were dispatched to deliver the Emperor's message in person to distant Japanese Army forces in China and in Korea, hoping thus to mitigate the shock. A clique of die-hards nevertheless attempted to assassinate the new Prime Minister, Admiral Suzuki Kantaro; but by 2nd September when the formal surrender ceremonies took place, the way had been smoothed.

Opponents of the dropping of the atom bombs sometimes claim that Japan was on the point of surrender. That claim is not upheld by subsequent revelations and a book called 'Japan's Longest Day', written by a group of fourteen Japanese historians of the 'Pacific War Research Society', (ISBN 0-87011-422-0, Kodasha International). The book shows how the cabinet was split equally and that after the Emperor had taken the decision to surrender, a group of officers attempted a coup to kidnap him, seize the recorded broadcast and force the Emperor to continue the war. The book, a paperback, is compelling reading.

THEN HIROSHIMA HAPPENED

Fred Seiker, Merchant Navy
(Continued from Part III)

Then HIROSHIMA happened! At dawn on 18th August 1945 I went on my usual trip to the latrines expecting the ritual early morning bashing from a guard for either not spotting him in time to bow, or bowing to an empty space whilst he was hiding a few yards away. But the bashing never came. No shouts of '*kurrah*'. Nothing stirred. There was an eerie silence. Others shuffled by, as bemused as I was.

I collected my mate and together we crept to the point where the guardhouse could be seen. Not a Jap in sight. Could this be a trap so that they would have the excuse of firing on us? The hated flag which usually hung draped at the bottom of the flag-pole after sundown had gone: there were empty crates and rubbish strewn all over the place. I remember we looked at each other in total disbelief. We entered into the open, every sinew in our bodies tensed, expecting the unexpected. Nothing happened. Still no Japs. Then someone shouted, 'The bastards have gone.' The words shot through the camp like a lit fuse. Then someone else shouted, 'The lorries have gone.' And so they had.

After a while a few natives appeared telling us with gestures and much excitement that the Japs indeed had gone during the night. Later we learned that the war had ended three days earlier on 15th August. We wondered whether the Japs had known. I cannot begin to tell you how this news was received by us. Some sank to their knees and prayed. Others just stood there, tears streaming down their haggard faces. A few were running around, wildly gesticulating and screaming.

I could not grasp the enormity of what had happened. I had become a person again as suddenly as it was ripped away from me all those years ago. I remember the feeling of triumph that swept over me. I had done it! I had outlived all attempts by Hirohito and his murdering thugs to kill me. But, above all else, I could say 'No' again to anything and anyone. It is called democracy and freedom. Believe me, it's worth fighting for. The present generation and generations to come around our world must be made aware of this so that they can guard their birthrights with all their might.

However, a heavy shadow hung over the camp that day because on 16th August, a day after the war had officially ended, an Aussie friend was bayoneted to death by the Japanese. Perhaps he knew more than we did. He made an escape bid and was promptly returned to the camp by members of a nearby hill tribe. It was believed that the Japs paid handsomely for this kind of enterprise. I only hope that his folk at home never found out.

There remains to tell you that we found a serviceable locomotive and some flat-tops on a nearby siding. We began our journey south with great care and little progress. Then, after only a short while, a cry from the leading flat-top pierced the quiet air. Our ordeal was over! It was a rescue train slowly steaming up the track towards us, two Red Cross flags flying at either side of the loco. The train had left a base camp a few days earlier, picking up survivors as it rattled up the track. They had been told about us, but did not know where we were, and had begun to fear the worst. I do not recall ever having been given so many pills and injections in one single day. But I do recall the warmth coursing through my veins on swapping jokes with the medics: the feeling of belonging among your own.

I was eventually taken to the field hospital in Kanchanaburi where we were once again separated into groups of nationalities. I did not cherish this at all. Life became pretty boring after that whilst waiting to be repatriated. I managed to join the Military Police Corps after a while which kept me reasonably occupied.

I must tell you about an episode in Kanchanaburi which has stayed with me ever since. We used to frequent a Thai cafe for drinks, snacks, and exchange news. The owner of the cafe had a little girl who had stolen our hearts, and mine in particular. This little girl fell seriously ill. The Thai doctor said that he did not have the necessary drugs to treat her and that, without those drugs, she would die. We dragged our own doctor to the cafe to examine this little girl with the Thai doctor in attendance. He confirmed the Thai doctor's findings and agreed that without the required drugs she would indeed die. But, under the military rules at the time, he could not supply drugs of any kind to the Thai population. However, we understood the 'wink and nod' and so I became a thief once more. A close record was kept of the use of the drugs until the course was complete. The little girl made a full recovery. I have never had the slightest feeling of guilt about the way those drugs were obtained. I felt it was our 'thank you' to those Thai people who had put their lives on the line in trying to help us whenever they could. Needless to say, once the news got around, the local people were ready to accept us as their rulers; or so it seemed. This was a truly joyous time.

The aftermath of the Railway atrocity affected POWs in different ways. Some showed minor problems, some were crippled for the rest of their lives. Others spent the rest of their days in hospital. Some suffered mental problems. A few could not handle the return to normal life and committed suicide, the most distressing fatality of all. Still others saw their marriage torn apart, often because of complete character change. I was one of the lucky ones. My problems were manageable, though they are still with me today.

The problems I had to deal with whilst working on the Railway were mainly chronic dysentery, intermittent malaria attacks, of which one was touch-and-go, minor beriberi and a small tropical ulcer which miraculously disappeared. These ulcers were the most feared of all. They caused horrible limb disfigurements and often required amputation without an anaesthetic! But there was always the malnutrition problem, causing such slaughter among the POWs. I finished up with an enlarged spleen and liver and a permanent disorder of my digestive system as a result of the years of dysentery. On the whole I have managed very well in contrast to many of my old comrades who have led lives of misery since their release from hell. I had a little difficulty in adjusting to normal living and was treated by a psychiatrist for a while. Within a year of returning to normality I was ready to face the world again, and that is what I did.

One incredible point I have in common with other POWs still alive: we still have nightmares after more than half a century of civilised living. It would seem that the brain does not forget however hard one tries to wipe out certain events. I can't make up my mind whether this is a good or a bad thing.

In winding up this talk about the Railway, I would like to acquaint you with some related subjects which still cause bitterness:

1. In October 1946, the then British Government sold the Thai section of the Railway together with most of the rolling stock to the Thai Government for the bargain price of £1,250,000. The bulk of this money was used to recompense the owners of rolling stock, locomotives and rails removed by the Japs from Burma, Malaya and the Netherlands East Indies. I leave you to judge the morality of this trade deal. It means that for every British corpse that lies buried in Thai soil, the then Government was paid about £190. Spread over the total of Allied dead, this came to about £70 per corpse. A comforting thought indeed for the widows, relatives and other loved ones who lost their men folk in the jungles of Thailand and Burma.

2. The Japanese individual responsible for the infamous biological trials carried out on Allied POWs and others was initially arrested after the war as a war criminal. He was soon released following a deal with the Americans. He was moved to the US where, by all accounts, he was given a major job with a leading pharmaceutical organisation.

3. Well-documented sources have revealed that the Japanese High Command ordered their forces to kill all Allied POWs the moment Allied soldiers would

set foot on Japanese soil. The 'Bomb' prevented the unthinkable. One should remember that this happened within our lifetime.

4. The San Francisco Peace Treaty of 1951 contained an escape clause in Article 26 of the Treaty allowing British POWs to claim compensation in excess of the £76.50 allocated to them by the terms of the Treaty. Britain waived a very large proportion of its claim in order not to cripple the Japanese economy at the time. A Foreign Office directive stated that no publicity should be given to this decision.

5. At this point I would like to draw your attention to an event that somehow did not make the headlines. During the latter half of 1944 and the early part of 1945 large numbers of Allied POWs were transported to Japan from various locations in the Far East. The ships used for this purpose did not carry any markings indicating the presence of POWs aboard. As a consequence, eighteen Japanese vessels were sunk by Allied action. The total number of POWs transported on these ships was around 15,500. The total perished was about 11,050. The great majority of these transports took place during the latter half of 1944.

And finally, some impressions and emotions I treasure. It is hard to explain, but in some way I feel privileged to have endured and experienced the Railway episode. It is given to few people to observe their fellow beings stripped of the trappings of civilisation. The raw nature of man soon emerges once the protective mantle of society is ripped away. I have observed men of immense stature in civilian life crumble like dry earth when confronted with issues affecting their own lives or that of their comrades: a truly pathetic and pitiful sight. On the other hand, there was a man who in *civvie* street was the headmaster of an elementary school, by appearance a typical man for this job. Bald-headed, with a fringe of hair around the back of his head. Slightly built, of small stature, walking with a slight stoop. Always polite, always civil. The Japs did not bother him. He used to say, 'It won't last forever, they cannot possibly win this war. Just hang on, and all will be right in the end.' Then one day on the railroad, I do not recall what happened, he jumped in front of a Jap who was beating a sick friend. He shouted at the thug that if he wanted to beat up someone, he should at least have the courage to pick on a so-called fit person. The Jap proceeded to do just that with great abandon. The schoolmaster received a terrible beating. We had to carry him back to the camp that night. This timid, friendly little man rose to be a giant of mental strength, a beacon for us all to follow. We were separated later on, and I have not heard from this marvellous man ever since. There are many examples like this, exposing human nature at its best and worst.

I firmly believe that nothing that life throws at an ex-POW who has endured the Thai-Burma Railway can ever be as bad. It is a useful thought to keep alive. Another episode of recent times will always be with me. During the VJ commemorations in 1995 I held an exhibition of paintings at the Bevere Vivis Gallery in Worcester depicting Japanese atrocities carried out on the Thai-Burma Railway. News of the exhibition soon got around and the media turned up in force. As a result, people came to the Gallery from all over the place and from all walks of life. The emotions released on looking at my pictures and, for the first time, understanding a little of what happened to their loved ones, was an experience almost beyond description. It was just overwhelming. There was a huge man, towering above the assembled viewers, standing in the centre of the gallery, his fists clenched and tears streaming unashamedly down his bearded face. His father had died on the Railway. His grave had never been found. All that remained was his father's name on a plaque. How can one ever forget such pain and emotion?

With this in mind, I shall now finish this talk with a few words based on the theme of the now famous words, 'When you go home, tell them of us and say: we gave our tomorrow for your today.' My words are these:

'...and, when I came home, I told them about us, the dead and the surviving.
They listened, they nodded, smiling, forgetting.
The widow held my hand, kissing me on the cheek, lightly,
Not to rouse the pain within and walked away, sadly, proudly.
Yes ... I told them about us, when I came home. '

SNAPSHOT

On the way home from Japan I had to spend weeks in hospital in Osaka, Okinawa, Manila, and Singapore where I witnessed the huge numbers of Allied troops already trained and prepared for the landings in Japan. Getting on for two million men and women were awaiting a passage home instead of being part of the attack on Japan. How many of them would have survived the taking of Japan and how many Japanese civilians would have perished in such landings? A great deal more than were the victims of the *Bombs.*

Part IX
Post Mortem

Chungkai Camp Cemetery, Spring 1944
In Spring 1944, deaths among men mostly under thirty years of age, were about twenty a day. - G S Gimson

INNOCENTS OF HIROSHIMA: EXPLODING THE MYTH
Roy S Bratby, Gordon Highlanders

There is the oft-repeated myth of 200,000 innocent people being killed. There were no innocent people in Hiroshima. The city was a beehive of war industry. Every home was involved in the manufacture of parts for planes, boats, shells, and rifles. Even bedridden and wheelchair patients were assembling booby traps to leave in the path of the American aggressors. Anyone manufacturing bullets is as guilty as the person who fires them and must be dealt with accordingly.

Hiroshima was the lynchpin in the defence of the western half of Japan. The 2nd General Army of Field Marshall Shunroku Hata, comprising over 50,000 troops, was stationed around the city. The headquarters of the infamous *Kempi Tai* of over 900 officers was situated in Hiroshima Castle. In the huge complex of the shipyard they were constructing battle ships, cruisers, destroyers, and submarines and the small one-man Kaiten submarines. The Mitsubishi Factory was making all types of tooling machinery. The Yoshikiwa Army Airfield contained a massive store of soldiers' equipment, a large gun store, warehouses full of aircraft spares and the Army-to-Navy complex. In Hiroshima Harbour were hundreds of small boats and one-man submarines fitted with explosive warheads. These were to be used by *Kaitens* (suicide sailors) to attack the ships of the expected invasion of Kyushu.

The authorities in Hiroshima knew that the city was bound to come under air attack as soon as the Americans held the airfield on Okinawa. Consequently they had constructed huge shelters throughout the city. Fire lanes had been bulldozed through the central areas of the city. These safety measures could have saved thousands of lives but when the aeroplane spotters saw only one aircraft they decided not to sound the alarm as it would interrupt the production of armaments.

It has been voiced many times that the Japanese would have given up and capitulated by November 1945 without the use of the atom bomb. This was a pipe dream. People have no idea of the determination of the Japanese nation to resist the invasion until everyone was killed. Field Marshall Hata decreed, 'When the invasion begins every man, woman and child will be armed.'

The Americans estimated that the small three-square-mile island of Iwo Jima would be over-run and captured within four days. It took four weeks. The cost in human life was enormous. The Americans suffered 25,851 battle casualties. The conquest of the sixteen-mile-long island of Okinawa was expected to take four weeks. It took three months. Over 200,000 Japanese died. Mass kamikaze attacks sank 400 ships and killed 9,724 naval ratings. The number of American GIs killed was 49,151.

All the Allied prisoners in Japan were engaged on war work. Our task was tunnelling into the hills surrounding Nagasaki. In this rabbit warren of passages the Japanese were storing kamikaze aeroplanes. With the wings folded back they were quite small and the Japanese seemed to be packing them in by the hundreds. In fact, after the war it was discovered they had 3,850 kamikaze planes. As we travelled back and forth to work we saw the women being trained. Many of them had bayonets fitted with bamboo shafts. Others were practising with hand grenades. Their task was to kill one American soldier. They were being shown how to hide in a manhole or a ditch or the undergrowth and wait for the unsuspecting Allied soldier. It was the type of warfare carried out by the Japanese on Okinawa and Iwo Jima.

The line-up for the defence of the Japanese homeland was massive. They had 2,000,000 regular troops, 2,300,000 battle-hardened soldiers being ferried over from China and 28,000,000 being trained. When President Truman asked General MacArthur how long it would take to overrun and defeat Japan the General replied, 'If they use the same guerrilla tactics as on Iwo Jima and Okinawa it will take about ten years.' President Truman was stunned.

I wonder why no one ever plants a tree for the innocent victims of Nanking? In a recent documentary a Japanese veteran soldier, Shiko Azuma, described the Army's advance into China, 'When we came to a village we raped all the women then killed everyone silently with the bayonet. We did this so the next village would not hear gunfire and then we could sleep without fear of attack. Also dead people tell no tales.' Another Japanese veteran, Shozo Tominaga, declared, 'When we came to Nanking most of the Chinese Army had escaped across the Yangtse River. It was decided then that we should kill every living person in the city. For three weeks we carried on with our rape and kill policy and the banks of the Yangtse became clogged with corpses for miles down river. The officers urged us on. We acted like animals. However, to kill everyone became so great a task, we were ordered to cross the Yangtse and move on against the Chinese. The landing-craft could not reach the riverbank and we were told to leap over the rotting corpses to reach the boat.'

In Singapore the Japanese carried out the same policy as in Nanking but to a far lesser degree. All the Malay, Indians and other nationals were spared. Thousands of Chinese, hands tied behind them with their own shoelaces, were pushed into the docks. Some time later we prisoners spent weeks hauling these bloated cadavers out of the docks with grappling irons and piling them on lorries to be taken away and buried.

The Singaporeans have now erected a huge four-pillared obelisk in remembrance of the thousands of Chinese murdered by the Japanese.

THE MANHATTAN PROJECT

In June 1942, the US War Department initiated a plan to create a 'super-explosive' by exploring the nuclear fission process. Scientists at the University of Chicago, one of the many research centres working on the Manhattan Project, first met with success in December 1942 when they achieved a self-sustaining nuclear reaction. The first experimental atomic bomb was detonated on 16TH July 1945 in New Mexico. While attending the Potsdam Conference, the last inter-Allied conference of World War II, President Truman gave permission to proceed with the bombing of Japan.

On 6th August 1945, a bomb code-named 'Little Boy' was dropped on Hiroshima at 8.15 am by the B-29 Enola Gay. Three days later at 11.02 am a bomb of a different kind, known as 'Fat Man', was dropped on the port of Nagasaki. The two bombs killed approximately 110,000 people, injured about the same number and left vast areas utterly destroyed. Other bombs were in readiness.

Had Japan not surrendered, the first wave of an Allied invasion of Japan would have taken place in November 1945 with 1.5 million combat soldiers and three million in support. A second invasion would have followed the following March. Allied troops would have suffered huge casualties while American casualties alone have been estimated at one million.

In a briefing to the US Army prior to celebrations for the 50th anniversary of the victory over Japan in World War II, Brigadier General J W Mountcastle, Chief of Military History for the US Army, explained the extent of the Japanese defence in the event of an Allied invasion. At sea and off-shore invading fleets would have encountered massive attacks by suicide-bombers and the remaining Japanese fleet of submarines and naval vessels would have been put into action. Defence plans included the use of bacteriological warfare and poison gas, engaging of the civil population in 'hit-and-run night attacks and suicide charges', and strengthening caves and underground developments.

Was the bombing of Nagasaki and Hiroshima justified? Brigadier Mountcastle claims that Allied firebombing prior to an invasion would have resulted in far greater loss of human life than from the two atomic bombs. "Do not forget too", he said, "that those in Japanese hands would have been liquidated no later than the moment that the first Allied soldiers set foot on the Japanese mainland."

JAPANESE A-BOMB

Peter McGill, The Scotsman in 1995

Few Japanese know that their own scientists were close to producing a nuclear bomb. Like most of his Japanese countrymen, Dr Tatsusaburo Suzuki is emphatically opposed to nuclear weapons. 'I firmly believe that sort of weapon should never be used again,' he says of the world's first atomic bombings of Hiroshima and Nagasaki. He visited both cities shortly afterwards and tells his audience: 'If you had been there, you would feel the same.'

But Dr Suzuki 83, is no ordinary Japanese nuclear disarmer. A distinguished physicist, during the Second World War he held the rank of Lieutenant Colonel in the old Imperial Army, one of the leaders of a top secret military project racing to develop Japan's own atomic bomb. If the team had been successful Dr Suzuki notes, the Japanese A-bomb would probably have been dropped on Saipan or Tinian Islands in the Pacific which US forces had recaptured in 1944 and were using as launch bases for devastating incendiary attacks on Japanese cities by B-29 bombers.

Dr Suzuki's candid account of Japan's secret nuclear warfare research, all records of which he was ordered to destroy in the closing days of the war, once again illuminates a familiar Japanese ambiguity - some would say hypocrisy - about the nation's wartime suffering. Every Japanese who can speak, hear and read, knows the horrors of Hiroshima and Nagasaki yet Japanese school textbooks never mention that Japan's military leadership was also planning to drop atomic bombs on American targets. The subject is also rarely broached by the Japanese media. Consequently very few Japanese know about it.

As the 50th anniversary of the dawn of the nuclear age looms closer, Japan's feverish attempts to build an atomic bomb before 1945 are also conspicuously absent from the reflections, arguments and analyses already published and broadcast around the world. Instead, the usual crop of questions, debated in the West for the past fifty years but given new currency by this year's official censoring of doubts from the Enola Gay exhibition on the Hiroshima bombing at the Smithsonian Air and Space Museum in Washington, once again dominate discussion. Was the United States leadership right at the time to test such a terrible weapon on Hiroshima, killing some 200,000, mostly civilian, by blast and radiation disease, and another 140,000 dead from the second atomic bombing of Nagasaki? Did the bombings end the war in the Pacific, saving many more American and

Japanese lives, or were they motivated by other reasons - to intimidate the Soviet Union or to justify the enormous cost of the Manhattan Project? Were they peacemakers or the perpetrators of atrocities?

In Japan it might easily be thought that the volume and depth of self-pitying about the bombings, most forcibly enshrined in the A-bomb museum to Japanese suffering in Hiroshima, leaves no room for unsettling moral doubt about what Dr Suzuki and his colleagues had in mind before August 1945. This ignorance of events was explained by one former officer in the Japanese Imperial Army, a retired businessman, who says that the real reason for the silence and taboo of the last decades surrounding Japan's secret A-bomb project was even simpler: it was simply because of 'Fear of the Right wing. They might kill you because it would make Japan look no better than America.'

The pre-war germ of Japan's designs on the A-bomb was the same as for Jewish émigré leaders of the future top-secret Manhattan Project in the United States and atomic science researchers in Nazi Germany: the charismatic circle around physics genius Niels Bohr in Sweden. Yoshio (1890-1951) the 'father of Japanese physics' studied under Bohr at the University of Copenhagen before returning to Japan in 1928. *The Kodansha Encyclopaedia of Japan* mentions that Nishina 'headed an atomic bomb development project' during the Second World War but does not elaborate. Two of Nishina's equally brilliant collaborators, Shinichiro Tomonaga (1906-1979) and Hideki Yukawa (1907-1981) were awarded the Nobel Prize for Physics after the war, yet one searches in vain in contemporary Japanese newspaper accounts of their distinction, and their obituaries, for their leading roles in the wartime A-bomb project. Yukawa, on the other hand, is cited as 'a most vocal spokesman for the cause of peace and the peaceful use of atomic energy.'

Dr Suzuki claims he knew nothing of either the Manhattan Project or the Nazi atomic research in Germany during the war, although it was 'suspected' that America was researching an atomic weapon from the 'total disappearance' of research papers on nuclear fission from American physics' research journals from 1940. Japan's supreme military commander, Emperor Showa (the posthumous name of Hirohito), never received any report from the Japanese A-bomb team, nor did Showa give any 'permission' to the team, nor sign any documents relating to it, according to Suzuki. (Since Suzuki complied with orders to destroy all documents about the project in 1945, this is impossible to verify.) 'The involvement of the Imperial household was rather limited,' he says.

However, 'The younger brothers of the Emperor, Prince Mikasa and Prince Takamatsu, were greatly concerned by the deteriorating combat situation and decided that if we continued with conventional warfare Japan would be defeated. They thought Japan 'may have to go nuclear,' says Suzuki. Prince Mikasa is usually considered a Sinophile and a strong 'pacifist' and in recent years has revealed his abhorrence at witnessing Japan's other secret weapons, 'research' in chemical and bacteriological warfare, in wartime Manchuria. The Chemical Defence Command Engineering Academy of China has recently stated that 94,000 Chinese were killed or injured by Japanese poison gas attacks from 1937-45, the Kyodo news agency reported last month.

The late Prince Takeda, first cousin of Emperor Showa, once told this writer that since Japan had been engaged in 'total war', he had supported, as an army officer dealing with strategy, the experiments into chemical and germ warfare - the latter by the infamous Unit 731 - and the efforts to develop a Japanese atomic bomb.

Dr Suzuki recalls that Nishina's A-bomb researchers totalled only 'about 50' and had a budget of only ten million - then equal to $2.5 million - compared to the Manhattan Project's 'manpower of 125,000 and budget of $2 billion.' The Japanese project succeeded in producing 'four to five kilos of uranium hexafluoride' which America was already manufacturing by the ton in late 1944 - but never managed to separate the Uranium 235 needed for an atomic bomb. 'We had a 210 ton cyclotron (in Korea which the Russians captured) while the American one was 3,000 tons,' Dr Suzuki notes ruefully.

He is quite willing to believe recent reports that President Harry Truman had approved contingency plans to drop eighteen atomic bombs from August to December in 1945 if Japan did not surrender, as America at the time had 'eight nuclear reactors' to produce the fissionable A-bomb material. 'I am glad only two bombs were dropped and no more.'

While stridently critical of today's huge arsenals of 'super nuclear weapons' Dr Suzuki is evasive about the A-bomb project on which he secretly worked. 'I am aware that during the war, people around the emperor advocated the use of atomic weapons, because if the bomb had been used against the United States it would have prevented the fire bombings.' Of Saipan, one of the intended targets, Dr Suzuki admits it had 'hospital ships and civilians on the island', but implies this was of a different moral dimension to the American atomic bombing of the two Japanese cities.

JAPAN'S EXPERIMENTAL BOMB

On the very day that the Bomb was dropped on Nagasaki, the Japanese carried out an experiment of their own. At dawn on that day, a small remote-controlled motor boat was sent against a small island off the Hungnam Coast in the Sea of Japan. The atomic explosion triggered off in that boat vaporised dozens of fishing boats and the occupants who happened to be there. Japan had experimented on its own people!

The ability of the Japanese to produce an atomic bomb of the power used by the Allies was out of the question, a major reason being the lack of sufficient uranium, although some had been mined in Korea. It was certainly true that an exchange of technology and a small amount of supplies between Germans and the Japanese had taken place. The German U-boat U234, carrying 1100 pounds of uranium oxide (enough for two bombs) on the way to Japan from Kiel, surrendered on the German collapse and was escorted into the naval base at Kittery, Maine, USA by a US Navy destroyer. On board the U-boat were two high ranking Japanese scientists returning to Japan who committed suicide before they could be interviewed. The Japs had hoped to harness at least one atom bomb to a kamikaze plane or sub to target a substantial American installation.

From Fulcrum, Newsletter of Japanese Labour Camp Survivors' Association,
Issue 50, Autumn 1996

"The end when it came was like a miracle: the sudden and unexpected cure for a fatal illness."

CHANGI EVENSONG

John L Woods (Jayell)

Changi Evensong, organised and conducted by the author, was performed on a number of occasions during internment by the Changi Glee Singers for whom the work was specially composed. It was broadcast from Singapore immediately after the release. John L Woods, or Jayell as he was known, a judge in Ipoh before and after the war, was interned in Changi Jail. When released he was so ill that it was necessary for him to spend a year in hospital. It was then that he composed the bulk of his literary work.

Around these prison walls which long ago
Became our home beneath the Rising Sun
Darkness has fallen once again and lo!
Another day is done.

As we depart to lay our heads to rest
And to resolve in sleep our mortal cares
Our thoughts are filled with those that we love best
As surely we fill theirs,

And for a while our present troubles cease,
Our hearts unite in prayer that one day all
May meet once more
In peace.

Also available from Cualann Press

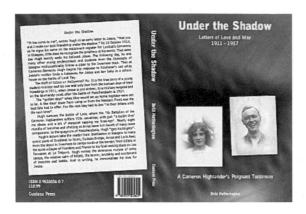

Under the Shadow
Letters of Love and War 1911-1917
The Poignant Testimony and Story
of
Captain Hugh Wallace Mann
7th & 5th Battalions
The Queen's Own Cameron Highlanders
and
Jessie Reid

Narrative: Bríd Hetherington

*"A sensitively-handled presentation, with introductions to each chapter
giving the background to events."* - The Scots Magazine

ISBN 0-9535036-0-7
£12.99
Voices of War Series

Cualann Press, 6 Corpach Drive, Dunfermline, Fife KY12 7XG. Scotland
Tel/Fax: 01383 733724 Email cualann@ouvip.com
Website http://users.ouvip.com/cualann/